Angler's Almanac: Conquering the Waters

Mastering Techniques, Choosing the Right Gear, and Exploring the World's Best Fishing Spots for the Passionate Fisherman

Benjamin Harlow

Summary

Chapter 1: Embracing the Passion for Fishing

Fishing, the age-old recreational activity, has captivated individuals throughout history. It has offered solace, excitement, and a chance to connect with nature's beauty. In this chapter, we delve into the world of fishing, exploring the allure, techniques, and the profound impact it has on passionate anglers. From the tranquil peace found by the water's edge to the adrenaline rush of landing a big catch, we unravel the mysteries and passion surrounding this beloved pastime.

The Call of the Water:

As the sun begins to rise, casting a golden hue across the horizon, nature awakens, and a symphony of sounds fills the air. Birds chirp their melodies, and fish begin their morning dance beneath the tranquil surface of rivers, lakes, and oceans. It is during these magical moments that the passion for fishing takes hold, and anglers all around the world are beckoned to the water's edge.

For many, fishing is more than just a hobby – it is an escape from the fast-paced, modern world, a way to reconnect with the whispers of nature. The rhythmic lapping of waves against the shore, the gentle rustle of leaves overhead, and the soft trickling of a babbling brook create a serene backdrop for the angler's meditation. Nature has a way of grounding our spirits, and fishing provides the perfect opportunity to immerse ourselves in this natural sanctuary.

The Beginner's Journey:

Each passionate angler begins as a novice, eager to learn the ins and outs of this ancient art. With a fishing rod in hand and a heart filled with excitement, they embark on a journey that often lasts a lifetime. The initial step is understanding the different types of fishing techniques and the unique requirements they demand.

Anglers can choose from a range of methods, such as fly-fishing, spinning, trolling, or baitcasting. Each technique has its own nuances, equipment, and rules, adding to the thrill of exploration. For beginners, it is crucial to start with the basics, mastering a single technique before diversifying their skills. Patience is an essential virtue, as the learning process involves trial and error, a delicate balance between technique, intuition, and adaptability.

Mastering the Craft:

As anglers progress on their fishing journey, they discover that fishing is not merely a matter of casting a line and hoping for a nibble. It is an intricate craft that requires a deep understanding of the fish's behavior, the allure of the bait, and the art of presentation. Seasoned anglers spend countless hours studying the sea's ebbs and flows, honing their skills in reading underwater currents and identifying prime fishing spots.

Beyond the practical aspects, fishing is also an art of patience and perseverance. Waiting for the perfect opportunity, knowing when to be still and when to move, requires a connection to nature and a harmony with the water. It is a delicate dance between angler and fish, an unspoken alliance formed between man and creature.

The Joy of the Catch:

In the pursuit of a successful catch, anglers immerse themselves in the rhythm of the water. They bask in the picturesque landscapes, savouring the beauty of their surroundings. But when the moment of action arises, and the fish takes the bait, an electrifying surge of adrenaline courses through the angler's veins.

The battle between angler and fish is a contest of strength and skill. The rod bends under the strain, and the line hums as the fish fights for freedom. It is a test of endurance, patience, and strategy. Finally, the victorious angler brings the fish to shore or into the boat. In that exhilarating moment, all the hours of dedication, practice, and love for the sport come together, resulting in an accomplishment that only passionate anglers can truly understand.

The Conservation Ethic:

To be a responsible angler means recognizing the importance of conserving the ecosystems that support the fish they so passionately pursue. Sustainable fishing practices, catch-and-release measures, and ethical treatment of the environment play a vital role in preserving the delicate balance of nature's aquatic habitats. Passionate anglers passionately advocate for the sustainability of fish stocks, ensuring that future generations can also experience the joys of fishing.

The Timeless Allure of Fishing

Picture this: It's a crisp morning, the sun is just beginning to rise, casting a warm glow over the calm waters. A slight breeze rustles the leaves on the trees that line the riverbank. You steadily cast your fishing line into the water, the anticipation of what lies beneath the surface building with each flick of your wrist. Fishing has captivated humans for centuries, and with good reason. It is a pastime that has stood the test of time, offering a unique and timeless allure that goes far beyond the mere act of catching fish. In this chapter, we explore the multifaceted reasons why fishing has such a profound and enduring impact on our lives.

The Call of Nature:

One of the most compelling aspects of fishing is its undeniable connection to the natural world. As humans, we often find solace and respite when we can escape the confines of our increasingly urbanized environments. Fishing allows us to immerse ourselves in the tranquility of nature, as we become one with the rhythm and flow of the water. The sights, sounds, and smells of the great outdoors awaken our senses, providing a much-needed reprieve from the noise and chaos of modern life.

Moreover, fishing allows us to experience a profound sense of connection with the natural world. Whether it's listening to the melodious chirping of birds, feeling the tug of the line as a fish bites, or simply basking in the stunning beauty of a sunset over the water, fishing empowers us to forge a deep and meaningful relationship with the world around us. It reminds us of our place in the grand tapestry of nature and brings us back to our primal roots.

The Thrill of the Chase:

Beyond its spiritual and meditative qualities, fishing also offers an exhilarating sense of adventure. When you cast your line, you enter a world of uncertainty, where anything can happen. Will you catch the biggest fish you've ever seen? Or will you encounter a legendary battle with an elusive creature that will test your skills and endurance? The thrill of the chase, the unknown that lies beneath the water's surface, is what keeps anglers returning time and time again.

Every fishing trip holds the promise of a new story, an unforgettable tale to recount to friends and family. Whether it's battling with a feisty trout in a rushing river or braving the treacherous waters of the deep sea in pursuit of a marlin, these adrenaline-fueled experiences create a lasting imprint on our memories. It is this unpredictability that makes fishing an addictive and enthralling endeavor for those who are brave enough to embark on it.

The Artistry of Angling:

Fishing, at its core, is an art form. Like a painter with a blank canvas, or a sculptor with a lump of clay, anglers use their tackle, bait, and technique to create their own masterpiece—a delicate dance between human skill and the natural world. The artistry of angling lies not only in the act of catching fish but in the intricate process that precedes it.

Choosing the right bait, understanding the behavior of different fish species, and honing the perfect casting technique are all essential components of becoming a skilled angler. It is a practice that requires patience, knowledge, and a deep connection to the water. Just as an artist can spend hours perfecting a brushstroke, so too can an angler spend years refining their craft, learning from both successes and failures.

A Bonding Experience:

For many, fishing is more than just a personal hobby; it is an avenue for building and strengthening relationships. Whether it's a father and son embarking on their first fishing trip, old friends rekindling their bond on a weekend getaway, or a couple finding solace in each other's company by the water's edge, fishing has an unparalleled ability to bring people together.

Shared experiences in the pursuit of fish foster camaraderie and a sense of unity. Time spent waiting for the fish to bite provides an opportunity for conversation, reflection, and the forging of new memories. The act of casting lines side by side, sharing stories and laughter, strengthens that bond even further. In a world often characterized by screens and virtual connections, fishing provides a tangible and genuine way of connecting with our fellow humans.

As dawn turns to dusk, and the day's fishing adventure comes to a close, one thing remains certain—the timeless allure of fishing endures. It is an activity that transcends time, cultures, and generations, deeply ingrained in the human psyche. From the enchanting allure of nature to the thrill of the chase, the artistry of angling to the bond it fosters between individuals, fishing offers something ineffable and innately human.

As you reel in your final catch of the day, take a moment to reflect on the magic of this timeless pursuit. Let the gentle lapping of the water against the hull of your boat or the whisper of the breeze through the trees remind you of the intrinsic connection we share with the natural world. Embrace the thrill of the chase, the artistry of angling, and the camaraderie it inspires. For within these moments lies the true essence of fishing—the timeless allure that keeps us coming back for more.

Nature's Call: Patience and Thrill

The wild has always held a mysterious allure, beckoning to the human spirit with promises of adventure and fulfillment. From the depths of dense jungles to the stunning peaks of majestic mountains, the beauty of nature captivates us. It is within nature's embrace that we encounter the duality of emotions - patience and thrill - drawing us deeper into its magnetic realm.

Patience is a virtue that nature teaches us, gently yet persistently. There is a certain harmony in observing the world around us, understanding that everything has its own rhythm and time. As I stand at the edge of an expansive savannah, the sun paints the horizon with hues of gold and orange, casting a warm glow upon the grasslands. The wisps of wind rustle through the tall grass, whispering tales of patience and resilience.

In the distance, a herd of elephants meanders gracefully, their colossal frames contrasting against the serene backdrop. These gentle giants command respect, reminding us that true strength lies not in aggression but in quiet fortitude. Watching their synchronized steps, I am reminded of the patience required to navigate the intricacies of life.

Each droplet of dew clinging to a delicate blade of grass holds within it the essence of patience. Birthed from the heavens, these tiny miracles slowly descend, nourishing the earth and breathing life into every living being. They remind us that nature's call does not adhere to the demands of man, teaching us to embrace the beauty of patience in our own journeys.

Patience finds its voice in the depths of the untamed oceans as well. As I embark on an underwater adventure, I am greeted by a mesmerizing dance of colors and creatures. Schools of fish dart through coral reefs, dancing in cadence with the currents. The coral itself is a testament to patience, a delicate masterpiece shaped by the relentless force of water over centuries.

Observing the intricate symbiosis between the species that call the reefs home, I witness the harmony born out of patience. The clownfish carefully navigate the fronds of anemone, while the gentle sea turtles glide gracefully, ensuring that balance is maintained. It is within the fragile ecosystem of the ocean that patience weaves its delicate tapestry, reminding us of the interdependence of all life.

Nature, however, does not solely beckon us with serenity and tranquility; it also whispers tantalizing hints of thrill. As I venture into the heart of a primeval forest, I am immersed in an eerie symphony of sounds. Rustling leaves, echoing cries, and the distant roar of mighty beasts intertwine, creating a crescendo of adrenaline and excitement. It is within this tangled wilderness that thrill is born, unfurling its wings in the face of the unknown.

Through the dense foliage, I catch a glimpse of amber eyes glistening in the moonlight. A tigress, exuding an aura of mystery and power, watches me intently. Her presence fills me with both fear and awe, reminding me that within nature lies the primitive force of the wild. The unpredictability of the wilderness is a catalyst for thrill, enticing us to embrace the unknown and step out of our comfort zones.

Climbing higher into the uncharted territory of rugged mountains, I find myself enfolded by their grandeur. Jagged peaks reach skyward, their majesty a testament to both nature's might and its allure. As I traverse treacherous trails, each step imbues a sense of exhilaration, reminding me of my insignificance against the backdrop of towering cliffs and expansive vistas.

Thrill pulses through my veins as I approach the precipice of a cliff, the abyss below barely discernible. The wind howls, kissing my cheeks with both a whisper and a roar. In this precarious moment, I feel alive - adrenaline surges through my body, and time seems to stand still. The thrill sought amidst nature's call reminds us of the invincible spirit that resides within each of us, waiting to be unleashed.

Nature embodies a paradoxical dance of patience and thrill, blending the gentle caress of tranquility with the electrifying pulse of uncertainty. It whispers tales of resilience and silent strength, urging us to embrace the ebb and flow of life. Amidst the enchanting landscapes and mystical horizons, we find ourselves at once humbled and exalted.

Embarking on this journey, nature teaches us to cultivate patience in a world plagued by haste and instant gratification. It unfolds the myriad wonders of the wild, allowing us to discover the thrill within ourselves. In the ceaseless pursuit of patience and thrill, we unlock the door to the untamed depths of our souls and uncover the magic that lies beyond the boundaries of our ordinary existence.

Join me as we delve deeper into the heart of nature, surrendering ourselves to its wisdom and enigmatic charm. Together, let us uncover the hidden stories woven within the fabric of our planet, exploring the delicate balance between patience and thrill that defines our relationship with the wild.

Ecological Harmony: Fishing's Impact

In our quest for sustenance and economic growth, humankind has long relied on the vast resources our planet has to offer. One such resource that plays a crucial role in feeding millions and sustaining coastal communities across the globe is fish. However, the impact of fishing on our fragile ecosystems is often overlooked, leading to the disruption of ecological harmony. This chapter delves into the multifaceted impact of fishing on marine environments, examining its consequences on fish populations, marine ecosystems, and the delicate balance that sustains life beneath the ocean's surface.

Fishing as a Livelihood

Since time immemorial, fishing has provided sustenance and livelihoods for numerous shore-based societies. For generations, communities have taken to the seas with their nets, lines, and boats to secure their food and financial stability. Fishermen honed their skills, passed down from one generation to the next, creating a bond between humans and the marine world. However, as populations grew, so did the need for more fish, triggering a significant transition in fishing practices and the introduction of modern vessels and technology.

Overfishing and Depleting Fish Stocks

The advent of industrialization brought forth an era of overfishing, as advanced technologies allowed us to harvest more fish than ever before. Unfortunately, this voracious appetite for marine resources has had dire consequences. Widespread overfishing has resulted in the depletion of fish stocks, causing a decline in species diversity and threatening the delicate balance of marine ecosystems. Popular fish species, such as tuna, cod, and salmon, face the imminent risk of collapse under the relentless pressure exerted by commercial fishing.

Bycatch: Unintended Victims of Fishing

Beyond the direct extraction of target species, fishing methods can have detrimental impacts on unintended victims - a phenomenon known as bycatch. As fishing nets trawl through the ocean, countless non-targeted species become ensnared, causing massive ecological disruptions. Sea turtles, marine mammals, seabirds, and countless other species are casualties of this unintended consequence. Bycatch not only contributes to species decline but disrupts the intricate web of marine life, as predators and prey become imbalanced.

Destructive Fishing Practices

Certain fishing practices, known for their destructive nature, exacerbate the impact on marine ecosystems. Bottom trawling, for instance, involves dragging large nets and heavy gear across the seafloor, resulting in the leveling of fragile habitats, such as coral reefs and seagrass meadows. These ecosystems provide vital nursery grounds, shelter, and spawning areas for numerous marine species, whose survival becomes jeopardized when indiscriminately destroyed by such practices.

The Role of Overfishing in Algal Blooms

The alteration of marine ecosystems caused by overfishing has far-reaching consequences, extending beyond the direct impact on fish populations. The decline of key predator species can lead to unforeseen ecological cascades, triggering an increase in algal blooms. Overfishing disrupts the natural checks and balances of marine environments, allowing certain algal species to flourish uncontrollably, blocking sunlight and depleting oxygen levels. These harmful algal blooms alter the composition of underwater habitats and have devastating effects on marine life, leading to mass mortality events and loss of biodiversity.

Depletion of Keystone Species

Depletion of keystone species, those disproportionately influential in the maintenance and balance of their ecosystems, is a critical consequence of overfishing. Notably, the removal of top predators, such as sharks and large fish, disrupts the function of entire food chains and creates a trophic imbalance. As populations of these keystone species decline, their prey proliferates, leading to the overconsumption of lower trophic-level organisms. This shift in ecological dynamics alters the structure and integrity of marine food webs, contributing to the overall disruption of ecological harmony.

The Socioeconomic Impact of Overfishing

The implications of overfishing extend well beyond ecological disruptions. Coastal communities reliant on fisheries for sustenance and economic stability are hit particularly hard when fish stocks collapse. As fish populations decline, fishermen face decreased catch rates, resulting in reduced incomes and food insecurity. Additionally, the loss of local fisheries can have profound cultural consequences, severing the longstanding ties between communities and their marine environments.

The Role of Aquaculture in Ecosystem Restoration

Though the impact of traditional fishing practices on marine ecosystems is undeniable, not all fishing activities are detrimental. Aquaculture, the practice of farming fish, presents an opportunity to alleviate some of the pressures on wild fish stocks while restoring ecological balance. Well-managed aquaculture systems can provide sustainable alternatives to wild fishing, reducing environmental impacts and providing a controlled environment for selective breeding and genetic improvement efforts. However, it is crucial to ensure that aquaculture practices are environmentally responsible and avoid exacerbating existing problems, such as pollution, disease transmission, and habitat destruction.

Solutions for Ecological Harmony

Achieving ecological harmony in the realm of fishing requires a multifaceted approach, combining efforts in conservation, regulation, and sustainable practices. Implementing strict fishing regulations and quotas, as well as creating marine protected areas, can help preserve fish populations and promote the recovery of depleted species. Exploring alternative fishing techniques that minimize bycatch and habitat destruction is another critical step toward ensuring sustainable fishing practices. Additionally, raising awareness among consumers about the importance of responsible seafood choices can catalyze demand for responsibly sourced fish, incentivizing the industry to embrace sustainable practices.

As we navigate the intricacies of balancing our need for fish with the preservation of marine ecosystems, understanding the impact of fishing is paramount. The chapter has shed light on the consequences of overfishing, bycatch, destructive practices, and the depletion of keystone species. By recognizing these challenges and collectively embracing sustainable fishing practices, we can pave the way toward achieving true ecological harmony, safeguarding the future of our oceans, and ensuring the longevity of both fish populations and the coastal communities that depend on them.

Seasonal Cycles and Targeted Species

When it comes to fishing, understanding seasonal cycles and targeting specific species based on those cycles is essential for several reasons, ranging from ecological conservation to maximizing the success of a fishing trip. Here's an explanation of the argument:

Behavioral Patterns of Fish: Many fish species have predictable patterns of behavior that vary by season. For example, certain species migrate to spawn, seek warmer waters, or follow their prey. By understanding these patterns, anglers can increase their chances of locating and catching fish.

Ecological Conservation: Some fish species are more vulnerable at certain times of the year, especially during their spawning seasons. Overfishing during these times can harm the reproductive success of these species and reduce their populations. Regulations often put restrictions on fishing during these sensitive periods to ensure sustainable fish populations.

Maximizing Catch Success: Knowing when a particular species is more active or abundant can increase the success rate for anglers. For instance, certain fish might be easier to catch during the spring when they're feeding heavily in preparation for spawning, while others might be more accessible in the fall as they fatten up for winter.

Gear and Tackle Selection: Different fish species require different gear and tackle. By targeting specific species based on seasonal cycles, anglers can equip themselves with the most effective gear, increasing their chances of success.

Safety and Comfort: Fishermen might prefer to target species that are active during times of the year when weather conditions are more favorable. For example, winter fishing might be productive for certain species but comes with challenges related to cold weather and potentially dangerous ice conditions.

Economic Considerations for Commercial Fishing: For commercial fisheries, understanding seasonal cycles can mean the difference between profitability and financial loss. Targeting specific species when they are abundant can result in a larger catch, which translates to greater revenues. On the other hand, fishing out of season might not only yield a smaller catch but also incur penalties or fines if regulations are violated.

Promotion of Diversity in Fishing: By promoting a varied approach to fishing, anglers are encouraged to learn about different species and the ecosystems they inhabit. This broader understanding can lead to a deeper appreciation of aquatic environments and the importance of their conservation.

Chapter 2: Techniques: A Fisher's Arsenal

In the vast and mysterious world of fishing, there lies a diverse array of techniques that anglers can employ to maximize their chances of hooking the catch of a lifetime. These techniques are the result of centuries of trial and error, passed down from generation to generation, constantly evolving and adapting to the ever-changing conditions of the aquatic realm. In this chapter, we shall explore the invaluable tools and strategies that constitute a fisher's arsenal, equipping them with the knowledge and expertise needed to thrive amidst the challenges of the waters.

The Art of Casting

At the core of every successful fishing expedition lies the skill of accurate casting. The ability to precisely deliver bait or lures to the desired location can make the difference between a bountiful haul and a disappointing outing. There are several casting techniques that seasoned anglers employ, each tailored to specific scenarios and fish species.

The overhead cast is perhaps the most widely recognized technique, wherein the angler propels the bait or lure forward with a smooth, fluid motion. This technique enables the fisher to cover great distances and is especially effective when targeting fish in open waters such as lakes or oceans.

Alternatively, the side cast is the go-to approach when navigating tight fishing spots characterized by dense vegetation or obstacles. By slinging the line to the side, the angler can avoid entangling the bait or lure in nearby objects, favoring accuracy over distance.

For those in pursuit of elusive freshwater game fish, the roll cast is an indispensable technique. It involves letting the line slide across the water's surface, resulting in delicate presentations that can entice even the most skittish fish.

Illuminating the World with Fly Fishing

A fishing technique steeped in tradition and elegance, fly fishing is an art form that has captivated anglers for centuries. Its roots can be traced back to ancient times, where humans observed the behavior of fish preying upon insects on the water's surface, thus inspiring the development of this unique method.

To be an effective fly fisher, one must possess an understanding of the insects that inhabit the waters they seek to conquer. Matching the hatch, as it is known, involves selecting a fly pattern that mimics the insects currently present. By doing so, the angler can heighten their chances of fooling even the wariest of fish.

The casting technique employed in fly fishing is markedly different from traditional methods. With a long and flexible fly rod in hand, the angler relies on the weight of the line to propel the fly towards their target. The delicate presentation entices the fish to strike, resulting in a truly exhilarating experience for the angler.

Be it in pristine mountain streams or sprawling rivers, fly fishing allows for a deep connection between angler and fish, beckoning individuals seeking a contemplative and serene encounter with nature.

Unlocking the Secrets: Trolling

When it comes to unlocking the secrets of the deep and targeting fish residing in the vastness of oceans and large bodies of water, trolling is a technique not to be overlooked. This method involves dragging lures, bait, or even artificial fish replicas behind a moving boat, imitating the motion of a live prey.

Many factors come into play when trolling, such as boat speed, lure selection, and the use of downriggers or planers to achieve desired depths. By varying these factors, anglers can effectively target a variety of species, from mighty marlins to voracious tuna.

Trolling allows for a degree of versatility unparalleled by other techniques. Whether it involves casting large skirted trolling lures, deploying live bait, or employing the use of attractants, this method provides anglers with exceptional control over presentation, enticing even the most finicky of fish to strike.

The Battle Beneath: Bottom Fishing

For those who prefer to keep their feet planted firmly on the ground, bottom fishing offers an enticing opportunity to engage in the age-old cat-and-mouse game with fish dwelling on the ocean floor. This technique primarily revolves around dropping baited hooks or weighted lures to the seabed, enticing fish that feed closer to the bottom.

Bottom fishing is a widely accessible technique suitable for both novices and experienced anglers alike. Patience is essential in this art, as a fish can take its time to inspect the bait before committing to a strike. It is often necessary to wait for the unseen hand to pull on the line, signaling a potential catch.

This technique has proven particularly fruitful for landing bottom-dwellers like groupers, snappers, and flounders. By adjusting the weight of the rig and the location of the bait, anglers can cater to the preferences and habits of specific fish species.

The World of Ice Fishing

In the frigid landscapes of northern regions, where frost-laden lakes become a frozen playground, ice fishing emerges as a unique and challenging pursuit. Anglers must exhibit both skill and patience as they drill holes through the ice, peering into the depths below in anticipation of their next catch.

Droplets of melting ice and whispers of breath hanging in the air create an atmosphere steeped in tranquility. Augers, manual or powered machines used to bore through the ice, become vital tools in this endeavor. Once the hole is made, anglers can employ a variety of techniques, including tip-ups and jigging, to lure unsuspecting fish in.

Tip-ups are simple yet ingenious mechanisms that are set up beside the hole. These devices, equipped with fishing lines and detachable flags, indicate when a fish has taken the bait, allowing anglers to respond swiftly and claim their prize.

Jigging, another popular technique, involves continually moving the bait or lure up and down, creating an enticing motion that tempts curious fish. The fisher can exercise control over the speed, duration, and depth of each jig, honing their approach to best suit the behavior of the fish below.

As we delve into the techniques comprising a fisher's arsenal, we are reminded that fishing extends far beyond the mere act of catching fish. It encompasses a profound connection with nature, a journey of exploration, and an everlasting pursuit of knowledge and skills. This chapter has merely scratched the surface of the vast possibilities and intricacies that anglers encounter in the watery domains. In the following chapters, we shall continue our quest, exploring different habitats, species, and the fascinating techniques employed to outsmart these underwater denizens.

Casting Precision and Distance

As an angler, mastering the art of casting is crucial to your success on the water. Casting with precision and distance allows you to effectively present your bait or lure to the fish, increasing your chances of a successful catch. In this chapter, we will explore the techniques, gear, and understanding required to improve your casting skills and achieve both precision and distance.

The Basics of Casting:

Before we delve into the nuances of casting, it is essential to grasp the fundamental principles. Casting is the act of propelling your fishing line and attached bait or lure through the air to a desired location. The primary factors that determine the success of a cast are accuracy, control, and distance.

Accuracy refers to the ability to place your bait or lure precisely where you intend, whether it be near submerged structure or in a specific area of a water body. Control is the skill of manipulating the line, rod, and reel during the cast to achieve the desired outcome. Distance, on the other hand, refers to the ability to cast your bait or lure far into the water, reaching those elusive fish lurking at a distance.

Perfecting your Technique:

To achieve both precision and distance in your casting, focusing on your technique is paramount. Several key components go into a successful cast, including stance, grip, rod loading, and release.

Stance:

Begin by adopting a balanced and stable stance. With your feet shoulder-width apart, distribute your weight evenly. This foundation allows for better control and prevents unnecessary strain on your body while casting.

Grip:

A correct grip on the fishing rod is vital for accuracy and control. The most common grip is the thumb-on-top grip, where your thumb rests on the top of the rod handle. This grip provides maximum control, allowing for precise adjustments during the cast.

Rod Loading:

Loading the rod refers to the process of building potential energy within the fishing rod, which is then transferred to the cast. To load the rod effectively, use a smooth and controlled motion, using your wrist, forearm, and shoulder in sync. This transfer of energy helps you achieve both distance and accuracy in your cast.

Release:

The release is the final moment of the cast and should be smooth and controlled. Avoid releasing the line abruptly, as this can lead to tangles or an inaccurate landing. Instead, release the line gradually and allow it to unravel freely for optimal results.

Understanding Gear for Casting:

Having the right gear is vital in achieving precise and distant casts. Different fishing rods, reels, and lines are designed for specific fishing techniques and conditions. Here, we will explore some of the essential factors to consider when selecting your gear.

Rod Action and Power:

Rod action refers to the flexibility and responsiveness of the rod, while power indicates its overall strength. Fast action rods have a more rigid tip, transferring energy efficiently and resulting in better distance casts. However, slower action rods offer greater precision and control. Select a rod action that best suits your casting style and fishing environment.

Additionally, choosing the appropriate rod power is crucial. Light power rods are suitable for finesse fishing and delicate presentations, while heavy power rods are best for ripping baits through dense cover or handling big game fish. Match the rod power to the specific fishing situation to optimize your casting performance.

Reel Selection:

The reel you choose should complement your casting goals. Spinning reels are often favored for their ease of use, versatility, and ability to cast with finesse. They are ideal for lightweight baits and lures.

On the other hand, baitcasting reels excel in casting heavier lures and baits, as well as in engaging big fish. They offer excellent control, allowing for precise presentations. However, mastering a baitcasting reel requires practice and precision in thumbing the spool.

Line Choices:

The fishing line plays a pivotal role in casting accuracy and distance. Monofilament lines are popular and versatile, with good casting capabilities. They offer excellent control and sensitivity, making them ideal for finesse fishing techniques.

Fluorocarbon lines, while more expensive, have a higher density and are nearly invisible underwater. These lines satisfy the need for stealthy presentations, especially in clear water fishing scenarios. Lastly, braided lines offer incredible strength and thin diameters. They are highly sensitive, have excellent casting distance, and are perfect for fishing situations that require long, accurate casts. Consider your fishing environment, target species, and desired casting performance when choosing the right line.

Environmental Factors:

Understanding and adapting to various environmental factors is crucial for casting precision and distance. Several conditions can influence how far and accurately you can cast, such as wind, water clarity, and obstructions.

Wind:

Wind can either be your friend or foe when it comes to casting. A tailwind can aid in achieving impressive casting distances. However, casting into a headwind can prove challenging. Adjust your casting position, technique, or gear accordingly to counter the effects of wind and maintain accuracy.

Water Clarity and Depth:

Water clarity and depth impact how fish perceive your bait or lure.

In clear water, fish may be more cautious and easily spooked. Distance casting allows you to keep a safe distance from wary fish and increases your chances of hooking them. Conversely, in murky or stained water, precise casting near structure or cover becomes more critical to elicit strikes.

Obstructions:

Whether it is shoreline vegetation, submerged logs, or overhanging branches, obstructions can impede your casting accuracy and distance. Familiarize yourself with your surroundings and adjust your casting trajectory and technique accordingly. Skipping casts or roll casts might be necessary to navigate around obstacles and ensure precise presentations.

Practice, Practice, Practice:

Casting precision and distance are skills that require practice and continual improvement. Committing to regular practice sessions will help refine your technique and deepen your understanding of the various factors that influence your casting success. Experiment with different techniques, gear, and environmental conditions to broaden your fishing capabilities.

Casting with precision and distance is an art that can be mastered through dedication, practice, and a deep understanding of the underlying principles. By focusing on your technique, gear selection, and adaptability to environmental factors, you will steadily enhance your casting skills and become a more effective angler. So, grab your rod, reel, and tackle box, head out to the water, and start honing your casting prowess. The rewards of accurate and distant casts await you, improving your chances of landing that trophy fish you've always dreamed of.

Luring Tactics and Natural Mimicry

Luring tactics and natural mimicry play a pivotal role in fishing. By imitating the natural food and behavior of prey, anglers can increase their chances of attracting and catching fish. Here's a breakdown of the strategies and the logic behind them:

1. Artificial Lures:

Plugs/Crankbaits: These are designed to imitate baitfish or other prey. They can float, sink, or stay suspended in water depending on their design. Their wobbling motion in the water can be irresistible to predators.

Soft Plastics: Imitating worms, grubs, and other aquatic creatures, these are often used for species like bass. Their soft texture can convince a fish that it's biting into a real organism.

Spoons and Spinners: Their shiny, reflective surfaces and movement imitate the flash of small fish, making them effective for attracting a variety of species.

2. Natural Baits:

Using live or dead natural baits can be very effective since they not only look but also smell and taste like the prey fish are accustomed to. Common natural baits include worms, minnows, crickets, and shrimp.

3. Mimicry in Motion:

Jigging: The act of lifting and allowing a lure to fall, imitating the motion of an injured fish or other prey. This motion can trigger predatory instincts in fish.

Retrieving: The speed and pattern in which a lure is reeled back can imitate various prey movements. For instance, a stop-and-go retrieval can mimic a wounded baitfish.

4. Color Selection:

Using colors that match local prey can be beneficial. For example, if a lake has a high population of bluegill, using blue and orange lures might be effective. Conversely, in clear waters or on sunny days, flashy or reflective lures can be more visible, while darker or more muted colors might work better in murky waters or overcast conditions.

5. Sound and Vibration:

Some lures, especially crankbaits, have built-in rattles. The noise can attract fish, especially in murky waters where visibility is reduced.

The vibration given off by certain lures, like spinners or vibrating blades, can be detected by a fish's lateral line, a sensory organ that detects movement and vibration in the water.

6. Surface Lures:

These lures operate at the water's surface, imitating injured fish, frogs, or insects. Their splashing and darting motions can entice fish to strike from below.

7. Scented Lures:

Some artificial lures are infused with scents that imitate natural prey or trigger feeding instincts, making them more appealing to fish.

The core principle behind luring tactics in fishing is the imitation of natural prey, both in appearance and behavior. By studying the habits and preferences of target fish species, and understanding the local environment and prey species, anglers can select and use lures that offer the best natural mimicry, increasing their chances of a successful catch.

Hook and Line Essentials

When it comes to fishing, the humble hook and line have been a mainstay for anglers for thousands of years. Dating back to ancient civilizations, this classic method continues to captivate the hearts of fishing enthusiasts around the world. In this chapter, we will explore the essentials of using a hook and line for fishing, examining the different types of hooks, lines, and techniques that can help you reel in that elusive catch. So grab your fishing rod and let's dive into the fascinating world of hook and line fishing!

Choosing the Right Hook:

The hook is the vital connection between you and the fish, and selecting the right type and size is crucial for success. Hooks come in a variety of shapes, sizes, and materials, each designed for specific fishing scenarios. Let's delve into the most popular types:

1. J-Hook: The J-hook is the go-to option for most anglers. Its simple design, characterized by a curved shank leading to an angled point, ensures a high hooking efficiency. Sizes vary depending on the targeted species, with smaller hooks suitable for panfish, and larger ones for saltwater fishing.

2. Circle Hook: Widely used in catch-and-release fishing, circle hooks are designed to prevent deep hooking and improve fish survivability. The rounded shape makes it less likely for the hook to embed in the

fish's throat, reducing injury. As the name suggests, the hook forms a circular shape, making it easier for the fish to take the bait fully before the hook sets.

3. Treble Hook: Comprising three hooks joined at a single eye, the treble hook is commonly used in lure fishing. It increases the chances of hooking a fish as it has three points to catch on. This hook is suitable for aggressive species or situations where quick hook sets are required.

4. Baitholder Hook: Often used for live or cut bait, the baitholder hook features two barbs on the shank to help secure the bait in place. This hook style is great for beginner anglers, as it provides extra assistance in keeping the bait intact and attracting fish.

Selecting the Perfect Fishing Line:

Beyond the hook, an angler's choice of line plays a vital role in hook and line fishing. Modern fishing lines are available in various materials, each with its own advantages and drawbacks. Here are the key types to consider:

1. Monofilament Line: Monofilament is the most widely used fishing line due to its affordability, versatility, and ease of use. This single-strand line is composed of nylon, and its low visibility underwater makes it an excellent choice for finicky fish. It also exhibits good knot strength and is less prone to tangling.

2. Fluorocarbon Line: Fluorocarbon fishing lines have gained popularity in recent years due to their near-invisibility underwater and superior abrasion resistance. Its density makes this line sink faster, allowing for more accurate bait control. Anglers often rely on fluorocarbon when targeting elusive fish species in clear water conditions.

3. Braided Line: Made from multiple woven fibers, braided lines offer exceptional strength and sensitivity. With a considerably smaller diameter compared to monofilament, braided lines have reduced visibility and allow for increased line capacity on reels. Their low stretch properties transmit even the slightest nibbles, giving anglers an advantage in detecting bites.

Reeling in Success: Hook and Line Techniques

Now that we have covered the basics of hooks and lines, let's explore some essential techniques that can enhance your chances of a successful fishing excursion:

1. Casting: Proper casting technique is fundamental to presenting your bait or lure in the desired location. Start by gripping the fishing rod firmly and extending your arm forward. With a fluid motion, release the line while pointing the rod towards your target area. Practicing different casting methods, such as overhead casting, sidearm casting, and flipping, is essential for accuracy and distance.

2. Setting the Hook: Once you feel a bite or notice a fish taking your

bait, you must set the hook swiftly to secure your catch. Depending on the hook type, gently raise or jerk the rod tip to embed the hook in the fish's mouth. Remember to maintain the right tension on the line to prevent the fish from unhooking during the fight.

3. Playing the Fish: After successfully hooking a fish, it's crucial to play it carefully to avoid line breaks or losing the catch. Keep a firm yet flexible grip on the rod, allowing the fish to make runs without putting excessive pressure on the line. Use the reel's drag system to control the fish's movements, adjusting the tension as needed. Patience and skillful rod manipulation are key to tiring out the fish while ensuring its safe landing.

4. Releasing the Fish: Fishing is not just about catching; it's also about conservation. Whenever possible, practice catch-and-release to contribute to the sustainability of fish populations. Handle the fish gently, ensuring its slime coat (a protective layer) remains intact. Use pliers or a hook remover to safely remove the hook, minimizing any harm to the fish. Finally, release it back into the water, allowing it to swim away with minimum stress.

From selecting the right hook to mastering essential techniques, hook and line fishing offers a captivating blend of artistry and skill. By understanding the various hook types, choosing the suitable fishing line, and employing effective techniques, anglers can significantly enhance their chances of success on every fishing expedition. So, embrace the simplicity and timelessness of hook and line fishing and embark on unforgettable adventures with nature's aquatic wonders.

Reeling Strategies and Landing Triumphs

In the world of fishing, there is nothing quite as exhilarating as the moment when you feel a tug on your line and know that you've hooked a fish. The battle between angler and fish is one that has captivated individuals for centuries, testing their skills, patience, and strategies. But what separates the average angler from the true masters of the craft? It is their ability to employ reeling strategies that allow them to land triumph after triumph. In this chapter, we will explore some of the most effective reeling strategies used by experienced anglers and discover the secrets to their success.

Understanding the Basics

Before we dive into the intricate details of reeling strategies, it is essential to establish a solid foundation by understanding the basics. The art of reeling begins the moment you feel a fish biting your bait or lure. It is crucial to remain calm, composed, and focused during this initial stage. Setting the hook with a swift, controlled motion can make all the difference in ensuring the fish remains hooked.

Once the fish is securely hooked, the next step is to assess its behavior. Different species and sizes of fish have unique tendencies when it comes to fighting. Some may immediately take off in a powerful surge, while others might exhibit a more subtle approach. Observing the fish's behavior and adjusting your reeling technique accordingly is essential for maximizing your chances of landing a trophy catch.

Pull and Reel Technique

One of the most widely used reeling strategies is known as the pull and reel technique. This technique involves a combination of exerting force on the fish while simultaneously reeling in slack line. By pulling the rod back and then quickly reeling in the line gained, anglers can maintain tension on the fish and prevent it from shaking the hook loose.

To execute the pull and reel technique effectively, it is crucial to synchronize the pulling motion with the reel handle rotations. The pulling motion typically involves a backward sweep of the rod, steadily but firmly applying pressure on the fish. As the rod is drawn back, the reel handle should be turned, reeling in the line gained during the pull. This allows the angler to maintain a constant tension and reduces the likelihood of the line going slack, giving the fish an opportunity to escape.

Anglers should be cautious not to exert excessive force when executing the pull and reel technique, as it could result in the line snapping or the hook tearing free from the fish's mouth. A delicate balance between applying pressure and allowing the fish to tire out is crucial for maximizing success.

The Art of Pumping and Reeling

When battling large or powerful fish, such as marlins, tunas, or groupers, the pump and reel technique becomes essential. This technique involves a combination of lifting the rod and reeling when the fish is drawing away and lowering the rod while reeling when the fish is swimming toward the angler.

The purpose of the pump and reel technique is to gain line on the fish while simultaneously tiring it out. By lifting the rod high and then lowering it, anglers exploit the fish's natural reaction of swimming away or towards them. This action creates a pumping motion that reduces strain on the angler while ensuring a constant pull on the fish.

It is crucial to maintain a rhythm when employing the pump and reel technique. Timing your actions to coincide with the fish's movement can significantly increase your chances of success. As the fish swims away, lift the rod and reel in line, applying steady pressure. As it approaches, lower the rod while reeling, carefully avoiding any slack in the line. This repetitive motion will gradually tire the fish and ultimately allow you to bring it closer to the boat or shore safely.

The Importance of Line Management

In the pursuit of reeling triumphs, anglers often overlook the critical aspect of line management. Proper line management can make a world of difference when it comes to landing a fish successfully.

One of the primary considerations in line management is maintaining the appropriate amount of tension on the line throughout the fight. Too much tension can lead to the line snapping, while too little can result in the fish shaking free. Adjusting the drag on your reel according to the fish's size and strength is essential for achieving the perfect balance of tension.

Furthermore, ensuring your fishing line is spooled correctly and free from tangles or knots is crucial. The presence of knots or tangles can weaken the line, making it more susceptible to snapping under pressure. Regularly inspecting and replacing worn-out or damaged line is essential to maintain optimal line strength.

Reeling in a fish is not simply a matter of luck; it is an art that requires skill, knowledge, and careful execution. Employing effective reeling strategies can dramatically improve your chances of landing triumph after triumph. By mastering techniques such as the pull and reel strategy, pump and reel technique, and paying attention to line management, you will be well on your way to becoming a formidable angler.

Remember, every fish you encounter will present its own unique challenges, and adapting your reeling strategies to suit their behavior is crucial. Continuously refining your skills and techniques through practice and learning from experienced anglers will ultimately lead to more successful fishing adventures. So, next time you find yourself in the midst of a battle with a trophy fish, confidently apply these reeling strategies, and prepare to land the triumph of a lifetime.

Chapter 3: Equipping for Success

Equipping for Success in Fishing

Fishing, at its core, is a dance between the angler and the aquatic world. However, it's not just about the dance; it's also about the stage, the backdrop, and most importantly, the attire. In fishing, your attire is your equipment, and to dance well, one must be dressed aptly.

Understanding Your Target

Imagine stepping into an arena without knowing your partner. That's akin to fishing without understanding the fish you're targeting. Each fish species has its quirks. Some might dart away at the slightest hint of danger, while others might be intrigued by certain movements in the water. Understanding these quirks is crucial, and it's the first step in equipping oneself appropriately.

A trout, for instance, might be more sensitive to line visibility, requiring the angler to opt for a clearer fluorocarbon line. A bass, on the other hand, might be attracted to the erratic movements of a crankbait. Thus, knowing your dance partner shapes the choices you make in your equipment.

The Backbone: Rods and Reels

The rod and reel are the extensions of an angler's arm. It's through these tools that one feels the subtlest nibbles or the aggressive tugs. But not all rods and reels are the same. A heavy rod might be great for pulling a massive catfish from the depths but would be overkill for the delicate art of fly fishing for trout in a mountain stream.

Furthermore, the reel's mechanism needs to complement the rod's purpose. The precision of a baitcasting reel might be favored by bass anglers, but someone chasing fast-moving fish in the ocean might prefer the rapid retrieve of a spinning reel.

The Allure of Baits and Lures

In the dance of fishing, lures and baits are the enticing moves that draw the fish in. The world of lures is vast, each designed to mimic some form of prey. But it's not just about looks. The movement, sound, and even scent can all play a part. Soft plastics wriggle like real worms, while certain crankbaits have built-in rattles to simulate the sounds of crustaceans. The key is natural mimicry—how well can an artificial lure imitate a living creature?

Tackling the Elements

Beyond the basics, an angler must be prepared for the external factors—the unpredictable elements. This includes understanding the effects of weather on fish behavior, equipping oneself with gear that can handle rain or cold, and even considering factors like UV reflections on sunny days which might require specific lure colors.

Embracing Technology

Modern fishing has seen a surge in technological aids. From fish finders that use sonar to pinpoint fish locations to drones that can scout vast water areas, technology has become a pivotal part of the angler's toolkit. However, it's essential to balance reliance on technology with intuition and experience.

Sustainability and Ethics

Being equipped for success is not just about catching the most or the biggest fish. It's also about ensuring that the aquatic ecosystems are preserved for future generations. This means using equipment and techniques that minimize harm to fish, such as barbless hooks or nets designed for safe catch and release.

In essence, fishing is a complex dance that requires more than just showing up. It demands preparation, understanding, and the right equipment. Only when all these factors align can an angler truly say they are equipped for success.

Selecting the Perfect Fishing Rod

Fishing is a passion that has captured the hearts of countless individuals around the world. There's something incredibly satisfying about casting your line and patiently waiting for your prize to take the bait. However, in order to have a successful fishing expedition, it is essential to have the right tools at your disposal. Among the numerous fishing equipment available, the fishing rod plays a crucial role in ensuring that your fishing trip is a fruitful and memorable one. In this chapter, we will delve into the world of fishing rods, exploring their various types, materials, and other important factors to consider when selecting the perfect fishing rod.

Understanding Fishing Rod Basics:

Before diving into the nitty-gritty details, it is important to have a basic understanding of the main components of a fishing rod. A typical fishing rod consists of the rod blank, grip, reel seat, guides, and tip. The rod blank is the main body of the fishing rod, responsible for transmitting the force to the fish. The grip is where the angler holds the rod, providing comfort and control during fishing. The reel seat holds the reel in place. Guides are small loops fixed along the length of the rod, guiding the fishing line to allow smooth casting and reeling. Lastly, the tip is the most flexible part of the fishing rod that allows anglers to detect and respond to bites.

Types of Fishing Rods:

When it comes to selecting the perfect fishing rod, understanding the different types available is crucial. Fishing rods can be broadly classified into three categories: spinning rods, casting rods, and fly rods.

1. Spinning Rods:

Spinning rods are the most popular and widely used type of fishing rods. They can be further divided into light, medium, and heavy rods, designed to accommodate different fishing styles and target species. Light spinning rods are perfect for catching small to medium-sized fish, such as trout or panfish. Medium rods are versatile and suitable for a wide range of fishing applications, including freshwater and saltwater fishing. Heavy spinning rods, on the other hand, are ideal for targeting large, hard-fighting fish, like saltwater game fish or freshwater catfish.

2. Casting Rods:

Casting rods, also known as baitcasting rods, are designed for more experienced anglers who prefer precision and accuracy in their casts. These rods feature a trigger grip and are specifically designed to handle heavier lines, lures, and bait. Casting rods are well-suited for targeting larger game fish like bass, pike, or catfish. Additionally, due to their casting mechanism, baitcasting rods offer better control and accuracy when casting under overhanging trees or into tight spots.

3. Fly Rods:

Fly rods are unique fishing tools primarily used for fly fishing, a specialized angling technique that involves casting artificial flies instead of bait or lures. These rods are typically longer and more flexible than spinning or casting rods. Fly rods are rated by "weight," denoted as a number ranging from 1 to 12, each designed for specific fly fishing scenarios. Lighter weight fly rods are suitable for small stream fishing, while heavier ones are used for big game fishing on large rivers or saltwater.

Factors to Consider Before Purchasing:

Now that we have explored the different types of fishing rods available, let's discuss the key factors you should consider before making a purchase.

1. Fishing Technique and Target Species:

The fishing technique you prefer and the target species you intend to pursue are crucial factors in determining the type of fishing rod you should choose. For example, if you enjoy casting lightweight lures into a river for trout fishing, a light spinning rod would be a suitable option. On the other hand, if you plan to troll for large game fish, a heavy casting rod would be more appropriate.

2. Rod Length:

Rod length plays a vital role in casting distance, line control, and sensitivity. Shorter rods generally provide better control and maneuverability, making them suitable for fishing in tight spaces or when targeting smaller fish. Longer rods, on the other hand, allow for longer casts, increased line control, and better leverage to fight larger fish. Consider the fishing conditions you typically encounter and the type of fish you aim to catch before determining the appropriate rod length for your needs.

3. Material and Construction:

Fishing rods can be made from various materials, including graphite, fiberglass, and composite materials. Each material has its own strengths and weaknesses. Graphite rods are lightweight, sensitive, and offer excellent casting distance, making them suitable for freshwater fishing. Fiberglass rods, on the other hand, are more durable and flexible, making them a popular choice for saltwater or heavy-duty fishing. Composite rods combine the best of both materials and provide a good balance between strength and sensitivity.

4. Power and Action:

The power and action of a fishing rod are two essential characteristics that greatly affect its performance. The power of a rod refers to its lifting capability and resistance to bending, ranging from ultra-light to ultra-heavy. The action of a rod describes how much of the rod flexes when pressure is applied, ranging from slow to fast. The power and action combination should be selected based on the target species and fishing technique. Light power rods with fast action are suitable for finesse fishing, while heavy power rods with medium action are ideal for casting heavy lures or bait.

5. Budget:

As with any purchase decision, your budget will play a significant role in the fishing rod you ultimately choose. Fishing rods can vary significantly in price depending on the brand, materials used, and overall quality. It is essential to find a balance between your budget and the features that are important to you. While premium rods often offer superior performance and durability, there are also excellent options available at more affordable price points.

Selecting the perfect fishing rod is a critical step towards enhancing your overall fishing experience. By understanding the different types of fishing rods, considering the fishing technique and target species, and evaluating factors like rod length, material, power, and action, you can make an informed decision that suits your fishing style.

Remember, the perfect fishing rod is not a one-size-fits-all concept but rather a unique combination of factors that caters to your preferences. So, delve into the world of fishing rods, experiment, and find the one that helps you reel in those memorable catches.

Lines and Leaders: Strength in Unity

Lines and Leaders: Strength in Unity in Fishing

The core of fishing success often boils down to the lines and leaders used, and when the discussion revolves around "Strength in Unity," it underscores how these components, when effectively combined, can determine the difference between a memorable catch and a lost opportunity. Here's an explanation of the argument:

Fundamental Understanding

Before delving into the intricate dance between lines and leaders, one must understand their basic roles. The main fishing line connects the reel to the hook or lure, while the leader is a short, often stronger or more invisible segment attached between the main line and the hook or lure. Together, they bear the brunt of a fish's fight, the underwater environment's challenges, and the angler's techniques.

Balancing Visibility and Strength

Fish are often wary creatures, especially in clear waters. The line, if too visible, can deter a fish from biting. Leaders, often made of fluorocarbon or monofilament, can offer low visibility, ensuring the fish only sees the lure or bait. However, a leader isn't just about invisibility. In environments with sharp rocks, coral, or toothy fish, a stronger, abrasion-resistant leader is vital. Thus, the combination of main line and leader offers a balance: the strength to fight and land a fish, and the stealth to not alert it prematurely.

Diverse Situations, Unified Solutions

Different fishing situations demand diverse line and leader combinations. For instance, when fishing for toothy species like pike or barracuda, a steel or heavy-duty leader is essential to prevent bite-offs. On the flip side, in the delicate world of fly fishing in clear streams, a thin, nearly invisible leader is crucial. In both scenarios, the unity of line and leader ensures optimal performance.

Knots: The Invisible Bond

The strength of a line and leader combo also heavily depends on the knots used to tie them together. A poorly tied knot can be the weak link that causes a setup to fail. Learning and mastering the right knots is essential to ensure the line and leader work in harmony.

Adapting to the Dance

Fish don't just bite and stay still. They run, they dive, they leap, and they twist. As an angler adjusts their techniques to the fish's moves, the line and leader must adapt without failing. Here, the synergy between the line's flexibility and the leader's strength becomes evident. While the main line might offer the elasticity to absorb sudden runs, the leader ensures that close encounters, especially near the boat or shore, don't result in break-offs.

Lines and leaders in fishing are a testament to the principle of strength in unity. Separately, they have distinct roles, strengths, and vulnerabilities. However, when unified effectively, they create a formidable combination, ensuring that anglers have the best chance at both enticing a bite and successfully landing their catch. It's a delicate balance, a dance of strength and subtlety, that underscores the art and science of fishing.

Optimizing with Fishing Accessories

Fishing is more than just a recreational activity; it is an art that requires patience, skill, and the right tools. While having the necessary fishing gear is essential, it is equally important to optimize your fishing experience by using the right fishing accessories. In this chapter, we will explore some effective fishing accessories that can enhance your fishing efficiency, increase your chances of success, and ultimately make your fishing trips more enjoyable. So, let's dive into the world of fishing accessories and discover how they can transform your fishing experience.

1. Fishing Line:

The fishing line is perhaps one of the most critical components of any fishing setup. When selecting a fishing line, you should consider its strength, visibility, and flexibility. Monofilament lines are versatile, affordable, and provide good knot strength. Braided lines, on the other hand, offer unmatched strength and sensitivity but can be less visible in the water. Fluorocarbon lines are virtually invisible underwater and have a high abrasion resistance, making them ideal for clear water applications. Understanding the properties of different fishing lines will allow you to choose the right one based on your fishing needs and conditions.

2. Fishing Reels:

Fishing reels come in various types, such as spinning reels, baitcasting reels, and fly reels. Each type has its advantages and is suitable for different fishing techniques. Spinning reels are easy to use and provide excellent casting accuracy, making them a popular choice for beginners. Baitcasting reels offer greater control and accuracy for targeting larger fish species, but they require more practice to master. Fly reels are specific to fly fishing and allow anglers to present flies accurately to fish in both freshwater and saltwater environments. Choosing the right fishing reel will contribute to the overall performance and success of your fishing outings.

3. Fishing Lures:

Lures are designed to mimic the appearance and movement of natural bait and are highly effective for attracting fish. There is a vast array of fishing lures available, each designed for specific fish species and fishing conditions. Hard-bodied lures, such as crankbaits and jerkbaits, imitate injured or fleeing baitfish and are ideal for predatory fish. Soft plastic lures, like worms and grubs, have a lifelike feel and are often used for targeting bottom-dwelling fish. Topwater lures create a commotion on the water's surface, enticing fish to strike. By understanding the behavior of the target species and selecting the appropriate lure accordingly, you can significantly increase your chances of a successful catch.

4. Fishing Hooks:

The fishing hook is the critical link between the angler and the fish. Ensuring you have the right hooks can make a significant difference in your fishing success. Hooks come in various sizes, styles, and configurations. When selecting a hook, you should consider the size of the fish you are targeting and the bait you will be using. Circle hooks are popular for catch-and-release fishing as they minimize injury to the fish due to their design. Treble hooks have three hook points and are commonly seen on crankbaits and other artificial lures. J-hooks are widely used for live bait fishing and offer excellent hook-setting capabilities. Using the appropriate hook will ensure that your catch stays hooked and increases their chances of survival when released.

5. Fishing Rods:

Fishing rods are available in different lengths, materials, and actions, and choosing the right one is essential for optimal casting and control. Shorter rods are ideal for close-quarters fishing, while longer rods provide greater casting distance. The material of the rod can affect its sensitivity and durability. Fiberglass rods are sturdy and can handle larger fish, but they may lack sensitivity. Graphite rods are lightweight and highly sensitive, making them suitable for detecting subtle bites. The rod's action, whether it is fast or slow, determines how much the rod flexes and influences the casting distance and the force required to set the hook. By selecting the appropriate fishing rod, you can optimize your angling experience and improve your chances of landing that trophy fish.

6. Fishing Nets:

A fishing net is an essential accessory for anglers of all skill levels. It allows for safe and efficient catch retrieval while minimizing the stress to the fish. When choosing a fishing net, consider its size, material, and design. Nets with large mesh sizes are suitable for landing large fish, while smaller mesh sizes are better for preserving delicate fish species. Nylon and rubber are common net materials that reduce damage to the fish's scales and fins. Additionally, collapsible nets are convenient for storage and transportation. Having a fishing net on hand will not only make landing your catch easier but also contribute to the fish's well-being.

7. Fishing Tackle Boxes:

Staying organized on the water is crucial for a successful fishing trip, and a tackle box is the perfect companion to store and organize your fishing accessories. Tackle boxes come in various sizes, designs, and configurations to accommodate different preferences. Look for a tackle box that has compartments or trays, allowing you to sort and store your hooks, lures, and other accessories conveniently. Some tackle boxes even come with built-in LED lights or transparent lids for enhanced visibility. By keeping your fishing gear organized and easily accessible, you can optimize your fishing experience and spend more time with your line in the water.

In this chapter, we have explored various fishing accessories that can significantly enhance your fishing experience. Fishing is not only about the thrill of the catch but also the art of optimizing your gear and techniques. From fishing lines and reels to lures and hooks, each accessory plays a significant role in increasing your chances of success.

By selecting the right fishing accessories based on your needs and fishing conditions, you can maximize your efficiency on the water and improve your ability to reel in that prized catch. Remember, investing in quality fishing accessories is an investment in your angling skills and the enjoyment of this timeless activity. So, gear up, get out there, and explore the incredible world of fishing accessories!

Chapter 4: Expedition to Prime Fishing Havens

The sun rose over the horizon, casting a warm golden glow across the pristine waters of the ocean. The salted breeze filled the air, lifting the spirits of the seasoned fishermen as they embarked on their long-awaited expedition to the prime fishing havens. These legendary spots were said to be teeming with an abundance of aquatic life, promising a bountiful and prosperous catch.

Led by Captain Benjamin Thompson, a weathered sailor with countless tales etched on his weathered face, the crew of The Sea Serpent had set sail towards uncharted waters, craving the thrill of adventure and the prospect of bringing home a record-breaking haul. The vessel, sturdy and brimming with supplies, was their trusted chariot in this grand journey. The crew, a mix of seasoned seafarers and enthusiastic apprentices, possessed an unbridled passion for the ocean and a steadfast commitment to their craft.

As the ship glided through the water, Captain Thompson gathered his crew around him on the deck, ensuring that a sense of camaraderie permeated every corner of The Sea Serpent. He addressed them with an air of confidence and authority that stemmed from years of experience. "We are embarking upon a noble mission, my friends," he began. "An expedition to the prime fishing havens, where legends come alive and dreams are forged. However, let's not forget the unpredictability of the sea and the ever-changing moods of nature. We must remain vigilant, adaptable, and forge our own path."

The crew nodded attentively, their eyes gleaming with determination. They knew all too well the challenges that lay ahead, from navigating treacherous waters to battling fierce storms. Buoyed by their unwavering spirit, they turned their gaze to the vast, open sea before them, anxious to explore the mysteries that awaited them beyond the horizon.

Days seamlessly turned into weeks, and The Sea Serpent gracefully navigated through the uncharted territories. Captivated by the breathtaking beauty that surrounded them, the crew encountered marine life that seemed to thrive in perfect harmony. Graceful dolphins glided alongside the ship, their playful acrobatics captivating the sailors and acting as a reminder of the intricate balance of life in the ocean. Majestic whales breached the surface, filling the air with their mesmerizing songs, while colorful schools of fish danced beneath them, a testament to the vibrant underwater kingdom they had stumbled upon.

Captain Thompson directed the ship towards the first of the many prime fishing havens they had planned to explore. The crew, armed with an arsenal of fishing gear, eagerly prepared for what lay ahead. Each member felt the weight of their responsibilities as they cast their lines into the water, hoping to feel the telltale tug of an eager catch.

The first few attempts proved fruitless, as the elusive creatures of the deep seemed to mock their efforts. But the crew, unperturbed, drew strength from their collective resolve. With each passing attempt, they gained insights, learning the nuances of the fishing hotspots and understanding the habitats of the elusive species they sought.

Day after day, the crew honed their skills, discovering new techniques and adopting innovative strategies. Their perseverance was rewarded with an increasingly impressive catch, their fishing nets bursting with an array of exotic species that dazzled the eye. Giant tunas, shimmering swordfish, and succulent red snappers all found their way into the hands of the eager crew, filling their hearts with pride and satisfaction.

As The Sea Serpent ventured further into unexplored territories, the crew encountered challenges that tested their mettle. They weathered violent storms that threatened to claim both ship and crew, dancing with the tempestuous seas and emerging stronger, having forged an unbreakable bond amongst themselves.

Amidst the relentless pursuit of their catch, the crew found solace in the serene moments that the open ocean bestowed upon them. Sunsets painted the sky with fiery hues, serving as a gentle reminder that even the most passionate of pursuits must be balanced with moments of contemplation and gratitude. Early mornings brought a peaceful silence broken only by the gentle lapping of waves against the ship's hull, instilling a deep sense of serenity within each sailor.

As The Sea Serpent approached its final prime fishing haven, the crew reveled in their achievements. They recounted tales of triumph and failure, preserving the knowledge they had gained to pass down to future generations of fishermen. Their expedition had not only secured a rich bounty, but also brought them invaluable experiences and lasting memories.

However, with every ending came a new beginning. The crew's focus shifted to their return journey, where they would carry their treasure trove of stories back to the safety of familiar shores. But as they prepared to set sail once more, they knew deep within their hearts that their expedition to the prime fishing havens had ignited in them an enduring love affair with the sea. It had lifted the veil on the wonders of the deep, reminding them of the importance of balance, perseverance, and the untamed beauty that awaited them each time they set sail.

And so, with full hearts and eager spirits, the crew of The Sea Serpent embarked on their homeward journey, forever changed by the majesty of the prime fishing havens they had discovered. Bound together by their passion for the sea and fueled by the memories they had forged, they longed for the next adventure that lay just beyond the horizon.

Global Fishing Allure and Local Wonders

The allure of fishing has captivated mankind for centuries, transcending cultures and continents. For many, it is not just a hobby or a means for sustenance; it is a profound connection to nature and a gateway to uncovering the wonders of the world's waters. In this chapter, we embark on a journey to explore the global fishing allure and discover the local wonders it unveils along the way.

1. The Intricacies of Angling

As we delve into the realm of angling, we find ourselves immersed in a world of skill, patience, and the harmony between man and water. It is a sport that demands understanding and adaptation to the ever-changing aquatic environments. From the breathtaking rivers of Montana to the remote lakes of Sweden, anglers embrace the challenge of coaxing elusive fish to bite the bait, each water body holding its unique treasures.

2. A Journey to the Amazon Basin

Join us now as we transport ourselves to the enchanting Amazon Basin, a realm renowned for its immense biodiversity and mysterious waterways. Here, fishing takes on an entirely new dimension as we encounter the legendary peacock bass, a brilliantly colored predator that tests even the most experienced angler's mettle. As we navigate the meandering tributaries, the calls of exotic birds and the rustling of lush foliage serenade us, creating an otherworldly experience that captures the essence of this remarkable destination.

3. The Icy Realms of Alaska

Leaving behind the equatorial warmth, we venture to the wild and rugged landscapes of Alaska. The allure of fishing in this icy wonderland lies not only in the prospect of catching trophy-sized salmon and halibut but also in the surreal beauty of the surroundings. The towering glaciers glisten under the sunlight while the orcas and humpback whales put on a mesmerizing display in the frigid waters. Here, fishing becomes a testament to human spirit, as we brave the hostile elements to partake in the bounty of the Last Frontier.

4. Tales from the African Waters

In the vast continent of Africa, where ancient traditions embrace a modern era, fishing offers a glimpse into the culturally rich lives of its inhabitants. We find ourselves tracing the footsteps of Hemingway, drawn to the shores of Lake Victoria, where Nile perch lurk beneath the surface. Casting our lines from traditional wooden boats, we engage in a timeless dance that connects us not only to the fish but also to the people who have depended on its bounties for generations.

5. Sailing the Mediterranean Seas

Our journey takes an unforeseen detour as we explore the Mediterranean, where angling is steeped in history and mythology. Embarking on a traditional fishing vessel, we traverse the cerulean waters, discovering hidden coves and ancient ruins along the way. Here, the Mediterranean's bounty showcases delectable species such as red mullet, sea bream, and the prized bluefin tuna, symbolizing a deep-rooted relationship between fishing and the culinary arts.

6. Unveiling Asian Mysteries

Moving eastward, we find ourselves in the mystical realms of Asia, where fishing has been elevated to an art form. The tranquil Zen gardens of Japan serve as the backdrop to our pursuit of the elusive cherry salmon. With meticulous precision, we engage in tenkara fishing, a traditional Japanese technique that exemplifies the simplicity and harmony between man and nature. From Japan, we wander to the vibrant shores of Thailand and Vietnam, where the rivers teem with exotic species like snakehead and Mekong giant catfish, luring intrepid anglers from around the globe.

7. The Delights of Home Waters

Closing our global fishing expedition, we return to familiar shores, reminding ourselves of the wonders that exist in our own backyards. Whether it's casting lines on a serene lake nestled in the heart of North America or chasing saltwater giants off the coasts of Australia, the allure of local fishing never fails to amaze. The shared stories and camaraderie formed between passionate anglers foster a sense of belonging and appreciation for not only the fish but also the fragile ecosystems they inhabit.

As we conclude this chapter, we are left with a profound realization that fishing is not merely the act of catching fish but rather an experience that unites people, cultures, and the natural world.

The global fishing allure unearths local wonders, unveiling the beauty and diversity of our planet's waters. From the awe-inspiring Amazon Basin to the tranquil lakes of our own neighborhoods, fishing takes us on a transformative journey, connecting us to nature, others, and ourselves. So, grab your fishing gear, cast your line, and embark on a voyage of discovery that will leave you forever captivated by the allure of the world's waters.

Planning: Permits, Stays, and Beyond

The allure of fishing is profound, promising serenity, thrill, and sometimes, an intricate game of strategy. However, behind every memorable fishing adventure lies a backbone of meticulous planning. The juxtaposition of a calm angler waiting by the water's edge with the rigorous preparation can be stark, and herein lies the premise for a deep dive into this argument.

The Ethical Foundation: Permits

Commencing the fishing journey without proper permits is like starting a book with its last chapter. Not only is it essential from a legal standpoint, but it underscores an angler's commitment to sustainable and responsible fishing. Permits:

Ensure Conservation: They contribute to local conservation efforts, ensuring fish populations remain healthy and thrive for future generations.

Determine Limits: Permits often come with guidelines on size and bag limits, ensuring anglers know what they can and can't keep.

Access: Some of the best fishing spots are regulated and only accessible with the right permits.

Laying Down Roots: Stays

Any seasoned angler would affirm that fishing isn't a mere daytime pursuit. It often extends into the early hours of dawn or the mystic veil of twilight. Choosing the right stay can:

Provide Convenience: Being close to the fishing spot can be advantageous, minimizing commute and maximizing fishing time.

Offer Amenities: Some lodges and cabins, especially those dedicated to fishing, offer specialized amenities like fish cleaning stations, guided tours, or boat rentals.

Ensure Rest: Fishing demands patience, and a good night's sleep or a quick nap can rejuvenate the spirit, enhancing the overall experience.

Knowledge Gathering: Local Insights and Weather

Entering a new fishing locale without understanding it is like reading a book in a foreign language. Gathering local insights and being aware of weather patterns is vital:

Local Expertise: Engaging with local guides or anglers can provide invaluable insights into fishing hotspots, techniques, and species-specific tips.

Weather Patterns: Fish behavior is heavily influenced by weather. Being aware of forecasts can help in choosing the right gear, timing, and location.

Equipment and Gear

While an angler's skill is paramount, being equipped with the right gear is just as critical. Planning involves:

Tackle Preparation: Ensuring that the fishing tackle is suited for the target species and water conditions.

Backup Gear: Always having spare gear, especially essentials like lines, hooks, and baits, can prevent unforeseen interruptions.

Beyond the Hook: Other Essentials

In the narrative of fishing, some elements, while not directly related to the act, can profoundly impact the experience:

Food and Nourishment: Long hours by the water require sustenance. Packing meals, snacks, and ample water is essential.

Safety Measures: First aid kits, communication devices, life vests, and even sunscreen can make the difference between a pleasant experience and a perilous one.

Environmental Respect: Equipping oneself with trash bags and adhering to a 'leave no trace' philosophy ensures the preservation of pristine fishing spots.

Freshwater Majesty: Rivers and Lakes

Imagine a world without rivers and lakes; a world devoid of the majestic beauty, abundant wildlife, and life-sustaining resources that these bodies of water provide. Rivers and lakes are not only important components of Earth's hydrological cycle, but they are also vital ecosystems that support a plethora of organisms, including humans. In this chapter, we embark on a journey to explore the awe-inspiring wonder of these freshwater bodies, delving into their origins, characteristics, the life they sustain, and the challenges they face in our ever-changing world.

Origins and Characteristics

Rivers, with their gushing waters and ever-flowing currents, have captivated human beings throughout history. They originate from various sources, such as melting glaciers, springs, and rainfall, and meander through diverse landscapes, shaping the terrain along their journey. As they carve their paths, they transform the surrounding environment, depositing essential sediments, nutrients, and organic matter. This continuous process of erosion, transportation, and deposition creates intricate natural features, including canyons, deltas, floodplains, and meanders, which are not only aesthetically stunning but also provide habitats for numerous organisms.

The unique qualities of rivers can be appreciated by examining their diverse characteristics. The width, depth, velocity, and volume of a river vary depending on factors such as precipitation, geology, and topography. For instance, the Amazon River, the largest drainage system in the world, flows with an average discharge of approximately 200,000 cubic meters per second, showcasing the sheer power and magnitude of a mighty river. In contrast, smaller rivers, such as the Rivière du Moulin in Quebec, Canada, boasts tranquil and crystal-clear waters, promoting biodiversity and providing a serene beauty that is equally captivating.

Lakes, on the other hand, possess their own allure and charm. Unlike rivers, lakes are relatively still bodies of water, formed by various geological processes such as tectonic activity, glacial action, and volcanic activity. Their size and shape can vary significantly, ranging from small, isolated mountain lakes to immense freshwater seas like the Caspian Sea. Lakes provide critical ecological services and are often considered as microcosms of the environments that surround them. They contain unique ecosystems and resources, contributing to the overall diversity and stability of the planet.

Life in Rivers and Lakes

Rivers and lakes are fertile habitats, teeming with a dazzling array of plants, animals, and microorganisms. These ecosystems support a complex web of life, where species interact with each other and the environment to create a delicate balance. At the foundation of freshwater ecosystems are aquatic plants like water lilies, reeds, and algae, which provide oxygen, shelter, and food for countless organisms.

Fish, amphibians, and reptiles are among the vertebrate species that call rivers and lakes their home. From the magnificent Nile perch of Africa's Lake Victoria to the elusive Amazon River dolphins, these waterways are a sanctuary for numerous aquatic creatures. Fish species like salmon undertake remarkable migrations, journeying upstream to spawn in the very rivers where they hatched. Amphibians, such as frogs and salamanders, rely on freshwater habitats for breeding, with their tadpoles metamorphosing into fully terrestrial creatures.

Birds are also drawn to the abundant resources offered by rivers and lakes. These bodies of water provide a source of food in the form of fish, aquatic invertebrates, and plants, making them ideal feeding grounds for waterfowl and wading birds. Magnificent species like herons, kingfishers, and the iconic bald eagle depend on rivers and lakes for their survival.

Challenges and Conservation

Unfortunately, the freshwater majesty of rivers and lakes faces numerous threats in our modern era. Pollution, habitat destruction, water extraction, invasive species, and climate change are but a few of the challenges that these ecosystems grapple with. As human populations grow, demands for freshwater resources increase, resulting in the overuse and depletion of these precious water sources.

Pollutants, both chemical and organic, find their way into rivers and lakes through industrial discharges, agricultural runoff, and improper waste disposal. These pollutants degrade water quality, harming the health of both aquatic organisms and humans who rely on these ecosystems. Harmful algal blooms caused by excessive nutrient inputs contribute further to the degradation of freshwater ecosystems, leading to fish kills and oxygen depletion.

Habitat destruction poses another significant threat. Wetland destruction, dam construction, and channel modification disrupt natural flows and reduce habitat availability for numerous species. These alterations often result in the loss of migratory pathways and breeding grounds essential for the survival of many animals, impacting not only their populations but also the intricate ecological balance of these ecosystems.

Conservation efforts are crucial to safeguard the freshwater majesty of rivers and lakes. Governments, organizations, and individuals worldwide are working together to restore habitats, regulate water usage, and monitor water quality. The preservation of riparian zones around rivers and the creation of protected areas, such as national parks and wildlife refuges, are steps in the right direction toward sustaining these invaluable ecosystems.

As we conclude this journey through the freshwater majesty of rivers and lakes, we are left in awe of the incredible beauty and importance of these ecosystems. Rivers and lakes are not mere bodies of water but intricate biological and geological wonders, shaping our planet and providing sustenance to countless species, including ourselves. It is our responsibility to cherish, protect, and conserve these invaluable resources, ensuring their preservation for future generations to marvel at the awe-inspiring wonders they hold.

Saltwater Splendor: Coastal to Deep-Sea

The ocean is a vast and mysterious world, teeming with a variety of lifeforms that have captured the human imagination for centuries. From the stunning beauty of coastal waters to the hidden depths of the open sea, the saltwater environment is a treasure trove of splendor waiting to be explored. In this chapter of our book, we embark on an awe-inspiring journey through the fascinating realms of marine life, from the enchanting coastal regions to the mysterious depths of the deep-sea.

Coastal Wonders:

Our adventure begins along the sprawling coasts, where the boundaries between land and sea blur to create an ecosystem teeming with diverse marine life. Coastal waters are often turbulent and influenced by tides, making them a haven for an astonishing array of organisms. Here, the rocky intertidal zones are teeming with life, acting as a constant battleground for survival.

Among the fascinating creatures inhabiting the rocky shores are the hermit crabs, scuttling along the tide pools and scavenging for food. These fascinating crustaceans, with their unique ability to inhabit shells discarded by other animals, exemplify nature's exquisite adaptability.

Venturing further into coastal waters, vibrant kelp forests come into view. These underwater oases are rich in biodiversity, serving as a refuge for a plethora of species. The towering kelp provides shelter for countless fish, sea urchins, and even marine mammals like sea otters. These captivating ecosystems are pulsing with life, as schools of colorful fish dart through the swaying kelp fronds.

Mangrove swamps, found along tropical coastlines, offer yet another glimpse into the marvels of coastal marine habitats. These unique environments feature mysterious root systems that emerge from the water's surface, creating intricate networks teeming with life. Mangroves provide nursery areas for juvenile fish, and their tangled roots provide a sanctuary for various species, including crabs and birds. The interplay between land and sea in mangrove swamps creates a captivating and dynamic ecosystem.

The Continental Shelf:
As we venture farther from the coast, we encounter the expansive continental shelf—a wide expanse of gently sloping seafloor that extends from the land edge to the continental slope. This area is characterized by shallower depths and abundant sunlight, making it a thriving region for marine life.

Coral reefs, among the most awe-inspiring marine environments, are found on continental shelves in tropical and subtropical regions. From the vibrant colors of the corals to the mesmerizing dance of the fish, coral reefs are truly a testament to nature's artistry. These complex ecosystems support an extraordinary diversity of aquatic life and provide protection and nourishment for countless species.

Descending deeper along the continental shelf, we encounter seagrass meadows, often referred to as the "forests of the sea." These underwater meadows are home to an astonishing range of organisms, from grazing sea turtles to tiny seahorses camouflaging among the seagrass blades. Seagrass beds play a crucial role in carbon sequestration and serve as vital nurseries for many commercially important fish species.

The Deep-Sea Realm:

As we continue our exploration, we transcend the relatively shallow realms of the continental shelf and venture into the abyssal plains of the deep sea. Light becomes scarce, and the overwhelming pressure of the depths renders this mysterious world seemingly inhospitable for life. However, the deep sea is home to resilient and peculiar creatures that have adapted to this extreme environment.

One of the most intriguing wonders of the deep sea is the mesmerizing bioluminescence that illuminates its inky darkness. Countless species have evolved the ability to produce light through chemical reactions, creating a captivating display of glowing organisms. From sparkling organisms like the vampire squid to glowing jellyfish drifting in the depths, the deep sea is a realm of enchantment.

Deep-sea trenches, like the Mariana Trench, are the most mysterious and least explored areas of the planet. These vast chasms go down to unfathomable depths, with pressures that are unforgiving to most living organisms. Yet even in these desolate environments, scientists have encountered remarkable lifeforms, such as the aptly named "snailfish," which survive in conditions that would be lethal to most other organisms.

As we come to the end of our chapter dedicated to the saltwater splendor of the coastal and deep-sea ecosystems, one thing becomes abundantly clear: the ocean is a realm of unfathomable beauty and magical diversity. From the vibrant coastal regions to the mysterious depths of the open ocean, marine environments captivate and awe us, revealing nature's astounding ability to adapt and thrive.

Our brief glimpse into this fascinating world only scratches the surface of what lies beneath. With so much left to discover, the ocean continues to hold endless secrets waiting to be unraveled. In our ongoing quest to unravel the mysteries of the ocean, let us never forget the privilege we have in being able to witness the saltwater splendor that exists within these enchanting realms.

Chapter 5: Conservation and Ethical Angling

In the pursuit of our passion for angling, it is imperative that we take responsibility for the conservation and preservation of our natural resources. Ethical angling goes beyond personal satisfaction and involves understanding the fragile balance of our aquatic ecosystems and the impact our actions can have on them. This chapter will delve into the importance of conservation in angling, exploring various practices and guidelines to ensure sustainable fishing for generations to come.

Understanding Ecosystems

Before discussing conservation, it is crucial to recognize the intricate web of interconnectedness within aquatic ecosystems. Rivers, lakes, and oceans are not just bodies of water; they are living ecosystems where countless species coexist and depend on each other. From microorganisms to fish and birds, each plays a vital role in maintaining the balance of these habitats.

By realizing the significance of our actions as anglers, we can contribute to the overall health and stability of these ecosystems. Conservation is not only about preserving fish populations but also about safeguarding the entire ecosystem on which they rely.

Understanding Fish Populations

To effectively conserve fish populations, it is essential to understand their life cycles and reproductive behaviors. Fish spawn, grow, and eventually reproduce, ensuring the continuation of their species. However, various factors can disrupt this delicate process, such as overfishing, habitat destruction, and pollution.

Overfishing

Overfishing remains one of the most significant threats to fish populations worldwide. Catching fish at a rate faster than they can reproduce depletes their numbers, disrupts the ecosystem, and compromises the delicate balance they contribute to. As ethical anglers, we must be aware of catch limits and practice responsible catch and release techniques.

Catch and Release

The principle of catch and release is a cornerstone of ethical angling. By carefully handling and returning the fish to their environment, we can help maintain their populations and ensure future opportunities for angling. However, it is crucial to handle fish properly during catch and release to minimize stress and maximize their chances of survival.

When pursuing catch and release angling, use barbless hooks or promptly remove the barbs to ease releasing the fish. Landing nets with rubberized, knotless mesh should be used to avoid causing injuries to the fish. Handle the fish gently with wet hands or a wet cloth, avoiding touching their delicate skin or gills. Lastly, release the fish in calm waters, away from structures or other potential dangers.

Habitat Preservation

Fish require suitable habitats to thrive and reproduce. As ethical anglers, we must make efforts to protect and preserve these environments. Habitat preservation involves various practices, such as avoiding destructive fishing techniques and being mindful of the locations we choose to fish.

Avoid destructive fishing techniques such as bottom trawling, as it not only destroys the fishing grounds but also harms the countless other organisms living in these habitats. Instead, use proper angling techniques that reduce damage to the environment, such as fly fishing or casting with artificial lures.

When selecting fishing locations, choose areas with minimal impact on sensitive habitats and consider biodiversity. Overfishing in a particular location can disrupt the balance of the ecosystem and potentially lead to irreversible damage.

Reducing Pollution

Pollution is a significant threat to aquatic ecosystems and the fish populations within them. Chemicals, plastics, and other waste have detrimental effects on water quality, disrupting natural habitats and impacting fish health. Responsible anglers must minimize their environmental footprint by adopting sustainable practices and promoting eco-friendly initiatives.

Never discard fishing lines, hooks, or any other waste into the water. These items pose significant threats to fish and other wildlife, causing entanglement and injury. Dispose of all fishing gear and waste responsibly, recycling whenever possible and ensuring proper disposal of hazardous materials.

Additionally, be mindful of the products you use while angling. Choose eco-friendly sinkers and lures made from non-toxic materials to prevent accidental ingestion by fish or other wildlife.

Educating Future Generations

Conservation efforts are not limited solely to our actions as individuals; they extend to educating others about the importance of ethical angling and environmental stewardship. By sharing our knowledge and experiences, we can inspire future generations to develop a deep appreciation for our natural resources and instill a sense of responsibility towards their preservation.

Engaging in community outreach programs, volunteering for habitat restoration projects, and supporting conservation organizations are valuable ways to contribute beyond our personal angling practices. Encouraging children and young adults to partake in fishing while educating them about ethical angling choices will ensure the continuation of responsible practices for years to come.

Conservation and ethical angling go hand in hand. As anglers, it is our duty to protect and preserve the environments and fish populations we cherish. By understanding the intricacies of our aquatic ecosystems, practicing responsible catch and release, preserving habitats, reducing pollution, and educating future generations, we can contribute to the long-term sustainability of our natural resources.

Through our combined efforts, we can continue to enjoy the thrill of angling for generations to come while ensuring the preservation of our precious lakes, rivers, and oceans.

Preserving Aquatic Ecosystems

The health and well-being of our planet depend on the preservation and proper management of its diverse ecosystems. Among these ecosystems, aquatic environments play a crucial role in supporting a wide array of life forms and providing essential services to both human and non-human communities. However, the ever-increasing human activities have put significant pressure on these delicate ecosystems, threatening their stability and the countless species that rely on them. In this chapter, we will explore the importance of preserving aquatic ecosystems, the threats they face, and the conservation strategies that can help ensure their continued vitality.

The Significance of Aquatic Ecosystems:

Aquatic ecosystems encompass a vast range of environments, including oceans, seas, rivers, lakes, wetlands, and estuaries. These ecosystems are not only home to an endless variety of species but also play a critical role in maintaining the Earth's overall balance. They are reservoirs of immense biodiversity, housing millions of species, some of which are yet to be discovered and understood. Moreover, they contribute to essential ecological processes such as nutrient cycling, carbon sequestration, water purification, and climate regulation.

The intricate web of life within aquatic ecosystems showcases a remarkable interdependency. Every organism, from the microscopic phytoplankton to the largest marine mammals, has a role to play in the functioning of these habitats. The complex interactions between species, such as predator-prey relationships and symbiotic associations, form the foundation of these ecosystems. The loss of even a single species can have cascading effects, destabilizing entire food chains and compromising the overall health of the ecosystem.

Threats to Aquatic Ecosystems:

Despite their immense ecological value, aquatic ecosystems face a multitude of threats due to human activities. Pollution, overfishing, habitat destruction, climate change, and invasive species are among the primary contributors to the degradation of these critical habitats.

Pollution poses a significant threat to aquatic ecosystems as it leads to changes in water quality and disrupts the balance of delicate ecosystems. Industrial and agricultural activities release vast amounts of toxins and pollutants into rivers, lakes, and oceans, causing water pollution. Chemical runoffs, oil spills, and excessive use of fertilizers lead to eutrophication, in which excessive nutrients in the water promote the growth of harmful algal blooms, depleting oxygen levels and threatening the survival of other organisms.

Overfishing, driven by the ever-growing demand for seafood, has resulted in the depletion of numerous fish stocks worldwide. Uncontrolled fishing practices, such as bottom trawling and the use of destructive fishing gear, not only harm the targeted species but also damage the habitats upon which countless other marine organisms depend. As a consequence of overfishing, entire ecosystems can face collapse, affecting the livelihoods of coastal communities and disrupting the food systems of nations that rely heavily on fish as a protein source.

Habitat destruction is another significant threat to aquatic ecosystems, particularly in freshwater environments. Deforestation, urban expansion, and the construction of dams and water diversion projects destroy the habitats of numerous species, disrupt the natural flow of water, and hinder migratory patterns. Wetlands, which were once abundant, have been extensively drained and converted for agriculture and urban development. These crucial ecosystems, acting as natural filters, are vital for water purification and flood control.

Climate change exacerbates the existing pressures faced by aquatic ecosystems. Rising temperatures, ocean acidification, and sea-level rise are all consequences of global warming, and they significantly impact marine ecosystems. Warming waters disrupt the delicate balance of coral reefs, leading to mass bleaching events that devastate the intricate ecosystems they support. Rising acidity levels in the oceans threaten the survival of calcifying organisms, such as shellfish and coral, while sea-level rise alters coastal habitats and increases the risk of coastal erosion and flooding.

Invasive species are also a growing concern for aquatic ecosystems. of non-native species, often due to human activities, can disrupt the ecological balance of a habitat and outcompete native species. Invasive species can alter the food web, reduce biodiversity, and cause the extinction of native species. Zebra mussels in the Great

Lakes and lionfish in the Caribbean are prime examples of the devastating impacts invasive species can have on aquatic ecosystems.

Strategies for Conservation:

Preserving aquatic ecosystems requires a multi-faceted approach involving local communities, governments, conservation organizations, and scientists. By implementing effective conservation strategies, we can mitigate the threats facing these delicate habitats and ensure their long-term survival. Here, we will explore some of the key strategies that have been successful in preserving aquatic ecosystems.

1. Establishing Protected Areas:

Designating protected areas, such as marine reserves and national parks, is essential for safeguarding aquatic ecosystems. These protected areas serve as havens for biodiversity, allowing for the recovery and flourishing of species. They also facilitate scientific research and provide opportunities for environmental education and awareness among local communities.

2. Sustainable Fisheries Management:

To combat overfishing, governments and fisheries need to work together to establish sustainable fishing practices. This involves setting catch limits based on scientific assessments, implementing gear restrictions, encouraging the use of selective fishing techniques, establishing no-take zones, and adopting measures that promote responsible fishing practices, such as the use of turtle excluder devices to protect endangered sea turtles.

3. Pollution Control and Remediation:

Efforts to control and minimize pollution are crucial for the preservation of aquatic ecosystems. Governments should enforce strict regulations and monitor the discharge of pollutants into water bodies. Encouraging the adoption of sustainable agricultural practices that reduce chemical runoff and embracing cleaner industrial technologies can help minimize pollution. Restoration projects should also be undertaken to remediate contaminated areas and improve water quality.

4. Habitat Restoration and Conservation:

Efforts should be made to restore and conserve critical habitats, such as wetlands, mangroves, and coral reefs. The restoration of degraded habitats promotes the recovery of biodiversity and the re-establishment of vital ecosystem services. This can be achieved through projects focused on reforestation, reef restoration, and the removal of invasive species that threaten native habitats.

5. Climate Change Mitigation and Adaptation:

Addressing climate change is crucial for the preservation of aquatic ecosystems. Governments must commit to reducing greenhouse gas emissions and transitioning to clean and renewable energy sources. Strategies should be developed to minimize the impacts of climate change on vulnerable ecosystems, such as developing marine protected areas that allow for species migration and promoting the adoption of resilient practices in coastal communities.

6. Public Education and Engagement:

Raising awareness about the value of aquatic ecosystems and the threats they face is essential for fostering a sense of responsibility among the public. Educational campaigns, outreach programs, and initiatives promoting environmental stewardship can empower individuals to take action and contribute to the conservation efforts. By fostering a deeper understanding of the interconnectedness of all living beings, we can inspire positive change for the preservation of these ecosystems.

Preserving the health of aquatic ecosystems is of utmost importance for the well-being of our planet and its inhabitants. By recognizing the critical role these ecosystems play and taking decisive action to address the threats they face, we can ensure their continued vitality. The preservation of aquatic biodiversity and the sustainable management of these delicate habitats will not only benefit countless species but also provide us with essential resources and services that form the foundation of our own existence. Let us stand united in our efforts to protect and preserve these magnificent aquatic ecosystems for generations to come.

Catch and Release Practices

In the world of recreational fishing, the practice of "catch and release" has gained significant popularity and recognition in recent years. This practice involves anglers catching fish and then releasing them back into the water, unharmed. While catch and release may seem like a straightforward concept, there is much more to it than meets the eye. In this chapter, we will delve into the principles behind catch and release, the benefits it offers, the proper techniques to ensure the fish's well-being, and its importance in preserving the delicate balance of aquatic ecosystems.

The Genesis of Catch and Release:

The concept of catch and release dates back centuries, although it has evolved over time. Early anglers often practiced catch and release out of necessity rather than choice, as they lacked the means to preserve their catches. As fishing techniques and equipment advanced, the focus shifted towards catching fish for sustenance rather than recreation. However, in the mid-20th century, recreational fishing started gaining traction, and catch and release began to emerge as an alternative approach.

The Ethical Implications:

Catch and release practices are rooted in ethical considerations. Anglers who choose this approach recognize the need to preserve fish populations for future generations and the ecological balance of aquatic ecosystems. By releasing fish unharmed, they contribute to maintaining healthy and sustainable fish populations, minimizing harm caused by overfishing, and ensuring the longevity of the sport itself.

The Environmental Benefits:

Catch and release practices have numerous environmental benefits, making them imperative to the conservation of aquatic ecosystems. One of the most significant advantages is the ability to reduce fishing pressure on certain species. Overfishing can lead to severe ecological imbalances, disrupting the food chain and causing irreversible damage to the ecosystem. Through catch and release, anglers can actively participate in the preservation of various fish populations, allowing them to reproduce and maintain their vital roles within the ecosystem.

The Impact of Selectivity:

Selective fishing practices are crucial to complement catch and release initiatives. Selective fishing entails choosing specific fish species or targeting a certain size range while avoiding vulnerable populations. This approach promotes the sustainability of fisheries, as it allows the larger, more mature fish to breed, ensuring healthier populations. By practicing selectivity, anglers indirectly contribute to the genetic diversity and resilience of fish populations, which are essential for adapting to changing environmental conditions.

Proper Catch and Release Techniques:

Implementing proper catch and release techniques is essential to minimize stress and injury to the fish, increasing their chances of survival post-release. Firstly, using appropriate fishing gear, such as barbless hooks, can significantly reduce harm to the fish. Barbless hooks are easier to remove and often cause less damage to the fish's mouth or gills. Furthermore, using artificial lures or flies when possible can reduce deep hooking, lessening the potential for serious injury to the fish.

Handling the Fish:

Once a fish is caught, proper handling practices must be employed to ensure its well-being. To begin, wetting your hands before touching the fish can prevent the removal of its protective layer of slime. This slime coat serves as a natural barrier against infection and disease, making it crucial for the fish's overall health. Additionally, handling the fish with wet hands or using a wet towel is recommended to minimize the potential removal of scales, which are vital for maintaining osmotic balance.

Unhooking the Fish:

The process of unhooking the fish is another critical aspect of proper catch and release practices. It is key to complete this procedure as quickly and efficiently as possible to minimize stress to the fish. If the fish is hooked deep, attempting to retrieve the hook using a tool specially designed to release fish can help avoid unnecessary damage. If the hook is embedded too deeply, it is best to cut the line and leave the hook in place, as attempting to remove it could cause severe harm.

Reviving and Releasing the Fish:

Once the fish is unhooked, it is crucial to support its body weight horizontally when handling it above the water's surface. Avoid holding the fish vertically, as this can strain its internal organs and potentially cause injury. Gently placing the fish in calm water, such as a net or the angler's hands, allows it to recover from the stress of being caught. Reviving the fish can be done by moving it back and forth in the water, generating a flow of oxygen over its gills, or gently moving it forward in the current. Once the fish shows signs of strong swimming and is responsive, it can be released with minimal harm.

The Role of Education and Awareness:

Raising awareness about the importance of catch and release practices is paramount to their success. Education programs, fishing associations, and governmental initiatives play a crucial role in disseminating information about the benefits and proper techniques involved. By educating anglers about the value of conservation, the vulnerability of fish populations, and the long-term impact of their practices, we can inspire a responsible fishing community and foster a culture of stewardship that extends beyond individual catch and release efforts.

Catch and release practices have become an invaluable tool in preserving fish populations and safeguarding the delicate balance of aquatic ecosystems. This chapter has highlighted the ethical implications, environmental benefits, and proper techniques associated with catch and release fishing. By actively promoting and practicing these techniques, anglers can contribute to the conservation of fish populations and ensure the continued enjoyment of the sport for generations to come.

Responsible Fishing Regulations

Fishing has been a fundamental part of human culture and sustenance for thousands of years. However, as our population grows, so does the impact of fishing on our oceans and marine ecosystems. Overfishing, destructive fishing practices, and the unsustainable exploitation of marine resources have led to significant declines in fish populations worldwide, threatening the long-term viability of our oceans.

To address these challenges, responsible fishing regulations play a crucial role in ensuring the sustainability of our marine resources. In this chapter, we will explore the importance of responsible fishing, the evolution of fishing regulations, and the key principles that underpin successful management strategies.

Historical Perspective

Throughout history, fishing regulations have evolved in response to changing social, economic, and environmental circumstances. Early regulations were often centered around local customary practices, which limited fishing capacity and protected spawning grounds. Indigenous communities, for instance, possessed an innate understanding of sustainable fishing practices and constructed their regulations based on this knowledge.

However, with the advent of modern technology and the rise of industrialized fishing, the need for more comprehensive fishing regulations became evident. The development of powerful fishing vessels, sonar technology, and the ability to locate and catch fish in greater quantities led to the rapid depletion of fish stocks. It became clear that a unified global approach to fishing regulations was necessary to protect our shared marine resources.

International Cooperation

Advancing responsible fishing practices required international cooperation and collective action. In 1995, the United Nations Food and Agriculture Organization (FAO) introduced the Code of Conduct for Responsible Fisheries. The code serves as a guiding framework for the development and implementation of fishing regulations, with a focus on maintaining the long-term sustainability of marine resources.

The concept of responsible fishing regulations embodies multiple principles, including protecting biodiversity, reducing fishing pressure, ensuring equitable access to resources, maximizing economic efficiency, and minimizing the environmental impact of fishing activities. These principles formed the basis for subsequent treaties, such as the 1995 Agreement on Straddling Fish Stocks and Highly Migratory Fish Stocks, which aimed to manage fish stocks that straddle both national and international waters.

Rebuilding Fish Stocks

One of the key objectives of responsible fishing regulations is to restore and maintain the health of fish stocks that have been overexploited. Many fish populations worldwide have experienced considerable declines, jeopardizing the long-term viability of these species and the livelihoods of those who depend on them.

To address this issue, fishing regulations commonly include strategies such as implementing catch limits, setting size restrictions, and establishing fishing seasons or closed areas. These measures allow fish populations to recover and rebuild their numbers, ultimately ensuring a sustainable supply of fish for future generations.

Monitoring and Surveillance

Responsible fishing regulations rely on effective monitoring and surveillance mechanisms to ensure compliance and deter illegal fishing practices. Modern technologies, such as satellite-based vessel monitoring systems, have greatly enhanced the ability to track fishing activities and detect violations.

By implementing comprehensive monitoring programs, fisheries management authorities can assess fishing effort, track catches, and enforce regulations more effectively. This enables them to identify trends, adapt management strategies, and mitigate the potential negative impacts of fishing on the ecosystem.

Bycatch Reduction

The unintended capture of non-target species, known as bycatch, is a significant concern in commercial fishing. Bycatch can include seabirds, marine mammals, turtles, and other fish species, many of which are endangered or protected. Responsible fishing regulations aim to minimize bycatch through the implementation of specific gear modifications, such as turtle excluder devices or specialized nets.

Furthermore, studies have shown that the use of selective fishing gear and practices can significantly reduce bycatch, ensuring the survival of non-target species. By promoting the adoption of these measures, fishing regulations can help preserve the delicate balance of marine ecosystems and protect vulnerable species from unnecessary harm.

Community Involvement

Responsible fishing regulations recognize the importance of engaging local communities, fishermen, and stakeholders in the decision-making processes. Combining traditional knowledge with scientific expertise, co-management approaches have been successful in many regions globally.

By involving local communities in fisheries management, responsible fishing regulations become more locally tailored, enhancing their effectiveness and acceptance. Additionally, empowering fishing communities and providing alternative livelihood options can reduce fishing pressure and support long-term sustainability.

Responsible fishing regulations are fundamental to the conservation and sustainable use of our marine resources. Through international cooperation, the adoption of principles outlined by organizations like the FAO, and the implementation of effective management strategies, we can protect and preserve our oceans for future generations.

In this chapter, we explored the historical perspective of fishing regulations, the importance of international cooperation, and the key principles underlying responsible fishing practices. Promoting the rebuilding of fish stocks, monitoring and surveillance, reducing bycatch, and involving local communities are all crucial aspects of responsible fishing regulations.

While progress has been made, it is vital that we continue to promote responsible fishing practices and adapt our regulations to meet the evolving challenges facing our oceans. By doing so, we can ensure the long-term health and abundance of marine resources for both environmental and economic benefits.

Balancing Recreation and Conservation

In today's fast-paced society, the need for recreation and the importance of conservation might seem like conflicting concepts. On one hand, humans are drawn to nature and the desire to disconnect from artificial environments, seeking solace in the great outdoors. On the other hand, it is essential to protect and preserve our natural resources to ensure their sustainability and safeguard the delicate ecosystems that support life on Earth. Balancing these seemingly opposing forces is crucial for creating a harmonious relationship between human recreation and conservation efforts.

Understanding Recreation

Before we delve into the topic of balancing recreation and conservation, let us first explore the concept of recreation and its significance in the human experience. Recreation encompasses various activities that individuals engage in for pleasure, relaxation, or enjoyment. It can take many forms, such as hiking, camping, fishing, wildlife observation, and even extreme sports like rock climbing or whitewater rafting. These activities provide opportunities for individuals to connect with nature and enhance their physical and mental well-being.

The Positive Impacts of Recreation

Recreation offers numerous benefits to individuals, communities, and society as a whole. It promotes physical fitness, encourages healthy lifestyles, and helps in reducing stress and anxiety. Engaging in recreational activities can also strengthen social connections, foster a sense of community, and boost overall happiness and well-being. Furthermore, recreation can be an educational tool, allowing people to learn about the environment, wildlife, and sustainability, and inspiring a love for nature that can translate into conservation action.

Understanding Conservation

While recreation focuses on personal enjoyment and well-being, conservation takes a broader perspective, looking at the long-term sustainability of our natural resources. Conservation involves the protection, preservation, and management of our environment, wildlife, and natural habitats. It aims to maintain the delicate balance between humans and nature, ensuring that future generations can also benefit from the resources that our planet has to offer.

The Need for Conservation

Conservation is vital for many reasons. First and foremost, it preserves biodiversity, safeguarding the wide array of plant and animal species that call our planet home. Biodiversity is essential for healthy ecosystems, as each species plays a unique role in them.

Additionally, conservation helps protect clean air and water, ensuring a sustainable environment for both humans and wildlife. Lastly, effective conservation measures can mitigate the impacts of climate change, preserving the delicate balance of our planet's systems.

Recreation and Conservation: A Delicate Balance

Finding a balance between recreation and conservation can be challenging, as the increasing demand for outdoor activities puts additional pressure on natural ecosystems. It is crucial to strike a delicate balance that allows people to enjoy nature responsibly while minimizing the negative impacts on the environment.

1. Education and Awareness

Education plays a vital role in achieving this balance. By raising awareness about the importance of conservation and teaching responsible recreational practices, individuals can make more informed choices. Providing educational resources, interpretive signs, and trained guides can enhance the visitor experience, enabling people to enjoy nature fully while respecting its limits.

2. Planning and Design

Proper planning and design of recreational sites and facilities are also essential. This includes considering the carrying capacity of an area, determining appropriate visitor capacity, and implementing infrastructure that minimizes environmental disruption. By designing well-thought-out recreational spaces, we can minimize erosion, disturbance to wildlife, and habitat destruction, allowing for recreation without a lasting ecological impact.

3. Sustainable Practices

Pursuing sustainable practices in recreational activities is another key aspect of balancing recreation and conservation. This can involve using eco-friendly equipment and materials, practicing Leave No Trace principles, and promoting responsible fishing and hunting practices. Minimizing waste, reducing your carbon footprint, and employing sustainable transportation options are all important steps toward environmentally conscious recreation.

4. Collaboration and Partnership

To achieve the delicate balance between recreation and conservation, collaboration between various stakeholders is crucial. Government agencies, environmental organizations, recreational enthusiasts, and local communities must work together to formulate sustainable management plans, establish rules and regulations, and enforce them effectively. By involving all relevant parties and considering diverse perspectives, we can develop inclusive strategies that preserve our natural resources while still offering recreational opportunities.

5. Monitoring and Adaptation

Monitoring and adapting management strategies is an ongoing process. Regular assessment of recreational sites, environmental impacts, and visitor behavior can help identify potential issues and adapt management approaches accordingly. This allows for continuous improvement in balancing recreation and conservation and ensures the long-term viability of both aspects.

Balancing recreation and conservation is a complex endeavor but a necessary one. As we navigate the challenges of an ever-evolving society, it is essential to remember that the joy and benefits of recreation should not come at the expense of our natural world. By implementing sustainable practices, raising awareness, and fostering collaboration, we can create a future where recreation and conservation coexist harmoniously, allowing both nature and humans to thrive.

Chapter 6: The Art of Fly Fishing

Fly fishing, often hailed as an art form, is a captivating sport that combines skill, patience, and an intimate connection with nature. As you delve deeper into this chapter, prepare to embark on a journey where the fly angler becomes one with the elements, stepping into a world where precision and finesse hold the key to success. In this chapter, we will explore the different techniques, equipment, and strategies employed by passionate fly anglers, showcasing the artistry that makes this timeless pursuit a deeply cherished endeavor.

1. A Brief History of Fly Fishing

Fly fishing has a rich and storied history, with evidence of its practice dating back over two thousand years. Ancient Roman and Greek cultures avidly engaged in fishing with flies made from natural materials such as feathers and horsehair. However, it was in the 15th century that fly fishing truly began to evolve into an art form, with the advent of more advanced techniques and an understanding of fish behavior.

2. Understanding the Fly

At the heart of fly fishing lies the fly itself - an artificial lure that aims to mimic various aquatic insects, small fish, or even larger terrestrial organisms. The fly is constructed using a combination of natural and synthetic materials, carefully selected to imitate the appearance and movement of its genuine counterparts. Understanding the different types of flies, such as dry flies, nymphs, and streamers, allows anglers to adapt their approach to the specific feeding habits of the fish species they target.

3. The Role of the Fly Rod and Reel

The fly rod and reel are vital tools that enable anglers to cast the fly accurately and control its movement through the water. Unlike traditional fishing, fly fishing relies on the weight of the line to propel the fly forward, rather than the weight of the lure itself. The fly rod, a long and flexible instrument, acts as a leverage mechanism, allowing anglers to exert control and manipulate the fly's presentation. Coupled with a well-balanced reel, the fly angler can expertly play, battle, and ultimately land their chosen quarry.

4. The Art of Casting

Fly casting is perhaps the most iconic aspect of this art form. Honing one's casting technique requires countless hours of practice to achieve the grace, elegance, and accuracy that define skilled fly anglers. The cast itself is a delicate dance, where the angler must employ a variety of motions to create an aerial loop of fly line, smoothly unfurling and delivering the fly to its intended target. Achieving a perfect cast, one that lands softly and naturally, is a testament to the relentless pursuit of mastery that is at the core of fly fishing artistry.

5. Exploring Different Fly Fishing Techniques

Beyond casting, a multitude of techniques exist for anglers to adapt their approach to prevailing conditions, fish behavior, and the specific environment they find themselves in. Whether employing dry fly techniques where the angler delicately presents a floating fly on the water's surface, or nymph fishing where the fly is submerged to mimic underwater prey, each technique possesses its unique challenges and rewards. Experienced fly anglers wield an extensive arsenal of techniques, ensuring they are prepared to adapt and triumph in any situation.

6. The Dance of Nature

Fly fishing not only requires skill and technique but also necessitates a deep appreciation and understanding of the natural world. The fly angler must become attuned to the intricacies of the environment - observing insect hatches, deciphering fish behavior, and reading the subtle movements of water. It is in this seamless integration with nature that the true magic of fly fishing unfolds - when the angler feels the rhythm of the river and moves in perfect harmony with the dance of life that surrounds them.

7. The Pursuit of Solitude

For many fly anglers, solitary pursuits are an integral part of the experience. The allure of remote rivers, tucked away in tranquil corners of the world, draws the discerning angler seeking refuge from the clamor of modern existence. The solitude found amidst pristine landscapes provides the space for introspection, inner peace, and an escape from the rat race. Fly fishing serves as a conduit, connecting anglers with the tranquility of nature, allowing them to find solace and respite from the hustle and bustle of everyday life.

8. Conservation and Fly Fishing

While the art of fly fishing encompasses personal satisfaction and enjoyment, it is equally important to recognize the role of anglers as stewards of the environment. The fragility of ecosystems and the delicate balance of aquatic ecosystems require responsible and sustainable practices. Fly fishing communities worldwide dedicate themselves to preserving natural habitats, protecting vulnerable fish species, and advocating for responsible fishing practices to ensure future generations may also experience the artistry of this revered sport.

Fly Fishing Origins and Philosophy

Deep in the heart of every fly fisherman lies a sense of wonder and reverence for the ancient art of angling. The delicate dance between the angler, the fly, and the elusive quarry dates back centuries, spanning cultures and continents. In this chapter, we delve into the origins and philosophy of fly fishing, seeking to unravel the timeless mysteries that have captivated generations of anglers.

1. The Origins of Fly Fishing

Fly fishing, as we know it today, is a culmination of a rich tapestry woven by various civilizations and their unique fishing techniques. It is widely believed that the practice originated in ancient Egypt, where drawings and writings on papyrus depict fishermen using long rods and feathers to imitate insects and entice fish to bite. These early attempts at fly fishing laid the foundation for what was to come.

The evolution of fly fishing continued in the Roman Empire, where the use of artificial flies made of feathers and colored wool gained popularity. The ancient Greeks also embraced fly fishing techniques, emphasizing the importance of a graceful, artful approach to catching fish. These early pioneers set the stage for future generations to refine the craft.

2. The Birthplace of Modern Fly Fishing: England

The birthplace of modern fly fishing can be traced back to England, where the sport truly flourished in the 19th century. English fly fishing enthusiasts, such as Frederic M. Halford and George Edward Mackenzie Skues, revolutionized the sport through their observations, innovations, and the publication of influential angling books.

Frederic M. Halford, known as the "Father of Modern Dry Fly Fishing," sought to imitate natural insect behavior through the development of meticulously tied dry flies. He emphasized casting accuracy, precise presentation, and delicacy, laying the groundwork for the highly artful and technical aspects of contemporary fly fishing.

G.E.M. Skues, on the other hand, challenged the predominant dry fly fishing ideology by advocating for the use of nymphs below the water's surface. His innovative techniques centered around imitating the subaquatic life cycle of insects, much to the dismay of many purists. Skues' contributions paved the way for what is now known as "nymph fishing" and expanded the angler's understanding of fish behavior and feeding patterns.

3. The American Influence

While England was the epicenter of fly fishing in the 19th century, it was in the vast wilderness of North America that the sport truly found its natural sanctuary. The United States, with its abundance of pristine rivers, lakes, and creeks, became a playground for anglers seeking solace and communion with nature.

Fly fishing in America was intimately tied to the development of trout fishing in the Rocky Mountains, particularly in the state of Montana. Pioneering individuals, such as Theodore Gordon and Charles Ritz, further popularized the sport. Gordon's observations and writings emphasized the importance of understanding the trout's natural habitat and behavior when designing effective flies.

Meanwhile, Charles Ritz, a French hotelier and fly fishing enthusiast, introduced the concept of "parachute fly" to the angling world. This innovative fly, characterized by a hackle parachute, allowed the angler to present the fly gently on the water's surface, mimicking a natural insect in its emerging or mating stage. Ritz's revolutionary design became a staple in fly boxes worldwide.

4. The Philosophy of Fly Fishing

At its core, fly fishing is more than just catching fish. It is a multifaceted pursuit that intertwines art, sport, and a deep connection to nature. The philosophy of fly fishing encompasses patience, observation, and a respect for the aquatic environment.

Anglers take pleasure not only in the actual catching of fish but also in the process leading up to the encounter. The act of refining casting techniques, selecting the perfect fly pattern, and reading the water's ever-changing currents becomes a meditative practice. The angler seeks to harmonize with the rhythm of the river, gaining a profound appreciation for the interconnectedness of all things.

Fly fishing's philosophy also extends to conservation and ethical angling practices. Many anglers adhere to the principles of catch and release, ensuring the long-term sustainability of fish populations. They become stewards of the environment, actively working to preserve the delicate balance of aquatic ecosystems.

Fly fishing is a captivating art form that has evolved over centuries, bringing joy, solace, and enlightenment to those who practice it. From its ancient origins in Egypt and the Roman Empire to its refinement in England and subsequent spread to North America, every chapter in the fly fishing story has added depth and complexity to this captivating pursuit. The philosophical aspects of the sport, emphasizing interconnectedness, patience, and conservation, elevate fly fishing beyond a simple hobby to a way of life. As we cast our lines into the shimmering waters, we honor the age-old traditions passed down through generations, perpetuating the timeless reverence for the art of fly fishing.

Fly Selection and Tying Techniques

The art of fly fishing is a delicate balance between science and artistry. The success of this angling technique hinges on the proper selection and presentation of flies. In this chapter, we will explore the intricacies of fly selection and discuss various tying techniques that every avid fly fisherman should have in their repertoire.

Fly Selection:

Fly selection is a crucial aspect of fly fishing, as different insects and baitfish attract specific fish species. To successfully mimic the natural prey and entice your target fish, it is essential to match the fly to the prevailing conditions and the preferences of the fish in question. Here, we will delve into the factors to consider when selecting flies for different fishing scenarios.

1. Matching the Hatch:

One of the fundamental principles of fly selection is the concept of matching the hatch. This involves selecting a fly that imitates the insects currently present on the water. Observing the hatching patterns and identifying the predominant species will help you choose the most effective fly pattern. This method is particularly useful when targeting trout, as they are notorious for being selective feeders.

2. Water Conditions:

Water conditions also play a vital role in fly selection. Factors such as water clarity, temperature, and flow rate can significantly impact a fish's feeding behavior. For example, during periods of high clarity, trout are likely to be more wary and selective. In such scenarios, it is recommended to use smaller and more realistic fly patterns. Conversely, in turbid or fast-flowing water, larger, more visible patterns may be necessary to attract fish.

3. Time of Day:

The time of day can dictate the type of insects present on the water's surface. Many aquatic insects are diurnal and have specific periods of high activity. Knowing these trends will help you choose the appropriate fly pattern for each time frame. For example, during the early morning or late evening, when mayflies are most active, using an imitation mayfly pattern can yield excellent results.

4. Seasonal Variations:

The seasons also have a significant influence on fly selection. Different insects hatch at specific times of the year, and as an angler, it is essential to familiarize yourself with these patterns. For instance, during the spring, stoneflies and caddisflies are prevalent, while summer brings an abundance of terrestrial insects like grasshoppers and beetles.

5. Fish Preferences:

Every fish species has its unique feeding habits and preferences. It is crucial to research and understand the predilections of your target fish. For trout, for instance, they might favor a particular type of fly, such as nymphs or dry flies, depending on the time of year or the specific stream you are fishing. Tailoring your fly selection to match the fish's appetite can significantly enhance your chances of success.

Tying Techniques:

Now that we have explored the importance of fly selection, let us delve into the various tying techniques that allow anglers to create their own customized flies. Tying your own flies not only adds a personal touch to your fishing experience but also provides the opportunity to fine-tune patterns to suit your specific fishing needs.

1. Basic Tools:

Before embarking on the art of fly tying, you must familiarize yourself with the basic tools of this craft. These include a fly tying vise, scissors, bobbin, hackle pliers, whip finish tool, and various types of hooks and materials. Having the proper equipment will make the tying process more efficient and enjoyable.

2. Understanding Materials:

Fly tying materials encompass a wide range of natural and synthetic components. These materials vary in texture, color, and buoyancy, allowing you to create a diverse array of fly patterns. Familiarize yourself with different materials such as feathers, furs, threads, and wires. As you gain experience, you will learn which materials work best for specific patterns and desired fly characteristics.

3. Nymph Patterns:

Nymph patterns imitate the immature aquatic insects that comprise a significant portion of a fish's diet. Tying effective nymph patterns requires an understanding of anatomy and the ability to create realistic imitations. Techniques such as dubbing, ribbing, and wing case construction are commonly employed to achieve the desired outcome.

4. Dry Flies:

Dry flies are designed to mimic adult insects that rest on the water's surface. Tying dry flies requires attention to detail and precise proportions to ensure the fly floats correctly. Techniques such as tailing, wing placement, and hackle selection are essential in creating a convincing dry fly pattern.

5. Streamer Patterns:

Streamer patterns mimic larger baitfish or other aquatic creatures such as leeches. These flies are typically larger in size and require different tying techniques to achieve the desired action in the water.

Tying techniques such as bucktail spinning and adding various weighted materials contribute to the lifelike movement and overall success of streamer patterns.

The art of fly selection and tying techniques is a worthy endeavor for any fly angler. Understanding the factors that influence fly selection, such as matching the hatch, water conditions, time of day, and fish preferences, can significantly increase your success on the water.

Equally important is mastering various tying techniques to create customized flies that accurately imitate natural prey. So, grab your vise, tie on, and embark on the wonderful journey of creating your own flies for a more exciting and successful fly fishing experience.

Reading Water and Identifying Targets

Water is an ever-changing element, fluid and elusive. It holds secrets and treasures within its depths, and as anglers, our ability to decipher its language is crucial to our success. Reading water and effectively identifying targets is an art that requires a keen eye, a deep understanding of fish behavior, and years of experience.

In this chapter, we delve into the intricacies of reading water, exploring the various factors that influence fish movement and behavior. From subtle surface patterns to underwater structures, we uncover the hidden cues that differentiate a productive spot from an unfruitful one. So grab your favorite fishing hat and let's dive in!

Section 1: Surface Clues

1. Ripples and Rings:

One of the first signs to look for when reading water is the presence of ripples or rings on the surface. These disturbances can reveal the location of feeding fish or indicate areas of underwater activity. Smooth, concentric rings often suggest that fish are rising to feed on insects, signaling potential feeding zones.

2. Current Breaks and Eddies:

Water currents play a vital role in fish behavior and can help you identify prime fishing spots. Look for places where the current changes speed or direction, creating breaks or eddies. These are often sheltered areas where fish can rest, ambush prey, or wait for food to come to them.

Section 2: Subsurface Structures

1. Rocks and Boulders:

Underwater structures, such as rocks and boulders, provide fish with shelter and create natural feeding zones. These hard structures attract prey, offering a perfect hiding spot for predators. Pay close attention to areas where rocks break the current flow or form small pools—these are often hotspots for hungry fish.

2. Reefs and Drop-offs:

Submerged reefs and drop-offs act as barriers and attract fish. Reefs provide shelter and food sources, while drop-offs offer depth variations that create ideal feeding grounds. As you scan the water's surface, keep an eye out for changes in color, indicating transitions from shallow to deep water. These can be potential target areas for trophy fish seeking an advantageous position.

Section 3: Vegetation and Aquatic Life

1. Plants and Weeds:

Underwater vegetation and weed beds are excellent indicators of healthy aquatic ecosystems. Fish love these areas as they provide cover, oxygenation, and abundant prey. Look for weed lines or clumps of vegetation close to the shore, as they offer an ideal hiding place for hungry fish waiting to strike.

2. Baitfish and Birds:

Where there's prey, there are predators. Keep an eye out for signs of baitfish and birds actively feeding in an area. Schools of baitfish are a good indication that larger fish are nearby, as they rely on these smaller fish for sustenance. Birds diving into the water or hovering above a specific spot signal a feeding frenzy, which means you should investigate further for potential fishing opportunities.

Section 4: Weather Conditions and Time of Day

1. Wind and Current Interaction:

Wind can dramatically impact water conditions, creating a ripple effect that can either attract or repel fish. When wind blows against the current, it creates a natural conveyor belt, funneling food and disoriented prey towards certain areas. These spots become prime targets for hungry fish. Conversely, wind blowing with the current can disperse food sources, making it harder for fish to locate and catch their prey.

2. Time of Day:

Different fish species have preferred feeding times, and understanding their patterns is critical. Many game fish are more active during low-light conditions, such as dawn and dusk. If you're targeting bass, for example, fishing early in the morning or late in the evening can increase your chances of success. Additionally, be mindful of water temperature variations throughout the day, as fish may move to different areas seeking optimal comfort levels.

Section 5: Angler Experience and Local Knowledge

1. Experience and Observation:

While it's important to learn the basics of reading water, experience and keen observation cannot be understated. As a seasoned angler, you'll develop a sense of fish behavior, honing your ability to recognize subtle nuances that others might miss. Pay attention to the smallest details, such as peculiar water movements or unusual bird behavior. With time, you'll be able to read water effortlessly and predict fish locations with greater accuracy.

2. Local Knowledge:

Every body of water has its own unique characteristics, and utilizing local knowledge can significantly boost your success rate. Local anglers, bait shops, or fishing guides can provide valuable insights into the best fishing spots, favored lures, and seasonal fish migrations. Even if you are fishing in a familiar area, don't dismiss the wisdom and expertise of those who spend countless hours on the water.

Reading water and identifying targets is an ongoing pursuit, blending science, intuition, and practice. It's a lifelong journey of discovery and learning, where each cast is an opportunity to unlock the secrets hidden beneath the surface. As you embark on your angling adventures, remember that patience, persistence, and an open mind are key ingredients to mastering the art of reading water and finding your next trophy catch.

Mastering the Cast: Delicacy and Precision

In the world of fishing, few skills are as crucial and rewarding as mastering the art of casting. Casting is not merely the act of throwing a fishing line into the water; it is a delicate dance that requires finesse, precision, and a deep understanding of the complexities of the fishing rod and the surrounding environment. In this chapter, we will explore the intricacies of casting, examining the fundamental techniques and key considerations that will elevate your casting abilities to new heights.

Section 1: The Anatomy of a Cast

Before delving into the nuances of casting, it is essential to understand the anatomy of a cast. A cast can be broken down into several distinct stages, each demanding careful attention and skill. Let us examine these stages in detail:

1. Loading the Rod:

Loading the rod refers to the process of storing energy in the fishing rod prior to casting. This is achieved by flexing the rod backward using your arm and wrist, allowing it to snap forward with a burst of power. Mastering the loading stage is pivotal, as it determines the distance and accuracy of your cast. Achieving a smooth, controlled load will set the foundation for a successful cast.

2. Accelerating the Line:

Once the rod is loaded, the next stage involves the acceleration of the fishing line. This is accomplished by gradually increasing the speed of the rod as it moves forward. It is vital to maintain control throughout the acceleration phase, ensuring a seamless transfer of energy from the rod to the line. Developing a smooth, progressive acceleration is key to achieving both distance and precision in your casting.

3. Timing and Release:

Timing and release are perhaps the most critical aspects of casting. As the rod reaches its maximum speed, it is essential to initiate the release, allowing the line to unfurl in the desired trajectory. The timing must be impeccable, with the release occurring just as the rod reaches its maximum forward velocity. A poorly timed or haphazard release will result in diminished casting distance and accuracy.

Section 2: Techniques for Delicate Casting

While distance and power are often prized in casting, there are moments when delicacy and precision are called for. Delicate casting is particularly essential when targeting smaller fish species, avoiding obstacles, or presenting a lure or fly with finesse. Here, we will explore three highly effective techniques for achieving delicate and precise casts:

1. The Roll Cast:

The roll cast is a fundamental technique that enables anglers to execute delicate presentations even when confined by surrounding obstacles or limited space. To perform a roll cast, the angler allows the line to settle on the water's surface, then initiates a gentle, rolling motion of the rod tip. This motion transfers energy to the line, causing it to unfurl and accurately deliver the fly or lure to the intended target. The roll cast is a valuable tool for casting under low branches, close to shorelines, or when presenting a fly in a gentle manner to easily spooked fish.

2. The Reach Cast:

The reach cast is a specialized casting technique employed to achieve precision when dealing with difficult currents or when presenting a fly naturally in a swiftly moving stream. To execute a reach cast, the angler performs a standard cast but extends their arm and body, allowing the line to unfurl downstream in a controlled manner. This technique creates a slight upstream curve in the line, enabling the fly or lure to drift naturally for more extended periods, deceiving wary fish. The reach cast is particularly useful when fishing for trout, as it offers a realistic presentation that triggers more strikes.

3. The Bow and Arrow Cast:

The bow and arrow cast is an invaluable technique when you find yourself in tight spaces with limited room for a conventional cast. This technique imitates the quick and accurate movement of an archer shooting an arrow. To execute a bow and arrow cast, you hold the line near the fly or lure, bend the rod back, and release it with a flick of the wrist. This propels the fly or lure forward with surprising accuracy and can be employed when targeting fish in confined areas such as dense vegetation, under bridges, or close to overhanging structures. Although it may take some practice to master, the bow and arrow cast is an indispensable addition to any angler's repertoire.

Section 3: Maintaining Casting Accuracy

Once you grasp the fundamentals of casting and have acquired the delicate techniques necessary, it is crucial to focus on maintaining casting accuracy. Fishing situations often demand precise casts to specific targets, and executing these casts consistently will undoubtedly increase your chances of success. Here are three essential tips to enhance your casting accuracy:

1. Practice Casts at Different Distances:

One of the most effective ways to enhance casting accuracy is to practice casting at various distances. Set up targets at different intervals and practice hitting each one with precision. By doing so, you will develop muscle memory, allowing you to execute accurate casts effortlessly regardless of the distance. Practicing different distances will also improve your ability to estimate and judge distances accurately, a skill that is vital when sight casting or targeting specific areas.

2. Minimize False Casts:

False casting is the act of repeatedly casting the line back and forth without presenting the fly or lure to the target. While it has its advantages, such as drying a waterlogged fly or preparing for a longer cast, excessively false casting can decrease accuracy. Each time the line is in the air, there is potential for error and decreased control. Aim to minimize false casts to only those that are necessary, allowing for more accurate and precise presentations.

3. Understand Wind Factors:

Wind can be both a friend and a foe when it comes to casting accuracy. Understanding the impact of wind on your casting and adjusting your technique accordingly is key. When casting into the wind, slightly overpower your cast to counteract the wind's resistance. Conversely, when casting with the wind, focus on maintaining precision by subtly adjusting your timing and release. Familiarizing yourself with the intricacies of casting in windy conditions will greatly enhance your casting accuracy, no matter the weather.

Mastering the art of casting is a lifelong journey, full of countless hours of practice and refinement. However, by understanding the anatomy of a cast, honing delicate casting techniques, and maintaining casting accuracy, you will undoubtedly elevate your skills to new heights. Remember, fishing is not solely about landing the biggest catch but about finding joy and fulfillment in the craft itself. Embrace the challenges, persevere through the setbacks, and with each cast, you will inch closer to becoming a true master of the cast.

Chapter 7: Navigating Different Water Bodies

Water bodies can be a mesmerizing and mystifying part of our natural world. From calm rivers to vast oceans, each body of water has its unique features and challenges. As humans, our curiosity has driven us to explore and navigate these water bodies for various purposes, such as trade, transportation, and even leisure. In this chapter, we will discuss the art of navigating different water bodies, understanding their dynamics, and the tools and techniques required for a smooth and safe journey.

1. Rivers:

Rivers are often considered the lifelines of civilizations, flowing through vast landscapes, connecting distant places, and providing essential resources. Navigating rivers successfully requires understanding their behavior and characteristics. Unlike open seas, rivers have defined courses, with varying depths and currents. A key navigational skill is reading the river's flow, identifying eddies and whirlpools, understanding the impact of tides, and learning to work with or against the current. Proper observation and knowledge of the river's channel markings, buoy systems, and lock systems are critical for safe navigation.

2. Lakes:

Lakes are tranquil bodies of water, often surrounded by picturesque landscapes. While their stillness may seem inviting, proper navigation in lakes requires careful consideration. One of the main challenges in navigating lakes is the presence of hidden obstacles such as submerged rocks or tree branches. Thorough understanding of the lake's topography, charts, and navigational aids is crucial to avoid mishaps. Additionally, knowledge of prevailing wind patterns, wave formations, and the impact of weather conditions on lake navigation is essential for a smooth journey.

3. Canals:

Canals are man-made waterways designed for various purposes, such as irrigation, transportation, and water supply. Navigating through canals presents unique challenges due to their narrow width and the presence of locks or sluices. The key to canal navigation lies in understanding lock operation, communicating effectively with lock-keepers, and maintaining proper etiquette when sharing narrow channels with other vessels. Since canals often have slower speed limits than open waterways, patience and careful planning are vital for an enjoyable journey.

4. Coastal Waters:

Coastal waters are a hybrid zone where the ever-changing dynamics of the sea meet the stable features of land. Navigating along coastlines demands knowledge of tidal patterns, changing currents, and potential hazards, such as sandbars or reefs. Understanding how to read nautical charts, interpret navigational aids, and utilize electronic navigation systems like GPS is crucial for safe coastal travel. Additionally, the ability to adapt to changing weather conditions, including fog, storms, and strong winds, is essential to ensure a successful journey along the coast.

5. Oceans:

The vastness of oceans has both captivated and challenged sailors throughout history. Crossing oceans safely requires meticulous planning, attention to detail, and a solid understanding of prevailing wind and current patterns. Navigating across open waters often relies on celestial navigation techniques, such as using the stars, sun, or moon for position fixing. Modern navigation tools, including electronic charts, radar systems, and satellite communications, have made ocean navigation more accessible and accurate. However, maintaining constant vigilance and having contingency plans in case of equipment failure remain critical skills for any sailor facing the open sea.

6. Inland Waterways:

Inland waterways encompass a diverse range of water bodies, including rivers, lakes, canals, and even small ponds. Navigating inland waterways requires versatility and adaptability due to the varying nature of these water bodies. Understanding the specific characteristics of each waterway, such as bridge clearances, lock systems, or speed limits, is essential to ensure a safe and seamless journey. Additionally, being mindful of environmental factors, such as nesting areas or protected habitats, is crucial for responsible and sustainable inland waterway navigation.

Navigating different water bodies is a fascinating and rewarding endeavor. Whether it be the steady flow of rivers, the stillness of lakes, the intricacy of canals, the ever-changing coastal waters, or the vastness of oceans, each water body presents its unique set of challenges and rewards. By understanding the dynamics, acquiring the necessary skills and knowledge, and utilizing modern navigational tools, sailors can confidently explore and enjoy the wonders of our diverse waterways. So, set sail, embark on your journey, and let the untamed beauty and majesty of water bodies captivate you.

Tricks for River Fishing Success

River fishing is an exhilarating and challenging endeavor that attracts many anglers seeking the thrill of the catch in a dynamic environment. However, it takes more than just casting a line and waiting for a bite to achieve success in river fishing. In this chapter, we will explore various tricks and techniques that will greatly enhance your chances of reeling in the big one. From understanding river dynamics to selecting the right bait, let's dive into the world of river fishing and discover the secrets to an unforgettable angling experience.

1. Get to Know the River:

Every river has its unique characteristics, and taking the time to understand its flow, structure, and species composition is essential for successful fishing. Begin your fishing expedition with some background research on the river you plan to fish in. Consult local fishing guides, online forums, and even talk to seasoned anglers who frequent the area. Obtain as much information as possible on the river's depth, speed, obstacles, and areas that are likely to hold fish. By developing a deeper understanding of the river's attributes, you can strategically position yourself to maximize your chances of a successful catch.

2. Observe the Water Currents:

Water currents play a significant role in river fishing. Along with influencing the location of fish, currents also impact their feeding patterns. Spend some time observing the flow of the river before casting your line. Look for areas where currents merge or split, as these are natural feeding zones for fish. Fish often gather near these confluences to capitalize on the influx of food. Additionally, pay attention to the speed of the current. Fish tend to congregate in areas where the water flow is slightly slower, providing them with a chance to rest and seek shelter from the main current.

3. Identify River Structures:

Rivers are home to various structures that attract and hold fish. Structures such as rocks, boulders, fallen trees, submerged logs, and undercuts offer shelter and act as feeding zones for fish. By familiarizing yourself with these structures, you can strategically present your bait to lure fish out from their hiding places. Cast your line upstream, allowing your bait to drift naturally towards these structures. Many fish species position themselves near these structures, waiting for an opportunity to strike at unsuspecting prey.

4. Understand Fish Behavior:

Understanding the behavior of the fish you're targeting is crucial for a successful river fishing adventure. Different fish species exhibit distinct behaviors, feeding patterns, and preferences. For example, trout prefer clear, oxygenated waters with rocky bottoms, while catfish often gravitate towards deeper, slower-moving waters with muddy bottoms. Once you've identified your target species, delve into their behavior patterns, feeding habits, and preferred bait options. Tailor your fishing approach accordingly, increasing your chances of enticing a strike.

5. Use Live Bait:

When it comes to river fishing, using live bait can greatly increase your chances of catching fish. Live bait presents a natural movement and scent that entices fish to strike. Popular live bait options include worms, minnows, crayfish, and insect larvae. Ensure that the live bait you choose is local to the river you are fishing in, as fish are more likely to recognize and be attracted to native prey. Always handle live bait with care and ensure that it remains fresh and lively throughout your fishing expedition.

6. Employ Artificial Lures:

While live bait is effective, artificial lures can also yield positive results in river fishing. Plugs, spinners, spoons, jigs, and soft plastic baits are all common choices for river anglers. The key is to match the lure's size, color, and action to the prevailing conditions and the fish species you're targeting. Experiment with different lures and techniques to find the combination that works best for you. Keep in mind that in river fishing, lures that mimic injured prey, like wounded baitfish or distressed insects, often evoke aggressive strikes from hungry fish.

7. Practice Proper Casting Techniques:

Casting your line accurately and efficiently is vital for river fishing success. In this dynamic environment, precise casts are often necessary to reach the desired fishing spots effectively. Mastering different casting techniques, such as the overhead cast, sidearm cast, and roll cast, will enable you to present your bait precisely where the fish are. Additionally, learn to cast against the current, allowing your bait to drift naturally and enticingly towards your target.

8. Vary Your Retrieve Techniques:

The way you retrieve your bait can make a significant difference in enticing a strike. Experiment with various retrieve techniques, such as steady retrieves, erratic jerks, or pauses, to mimic the behavior of injured prey. Fish, especially predatory species, are often triggered by sudden movements, erratic actions, or the appearance of vulnerability in their potential prey. By varying your retrieve techniques, you increase the chances of attracting the attention of fish and triggering a strike.

9. Be Mindful of Weather and Water Conditions:

Weather conditions and water temperature can greatly influence fish feeding behavior. Different fish species have different preferences regarding water temperature and clarity. Warmer water temperatures often lead to increased fish activity, while colder water temperatures tend to slow fish metabolism. Keep an eye on the weather forecast and select the best times to fish based on the prevailing conditions. Additionally, be aware of sudden changes in weather, such as rainstorms or fluctuations in air pressure, as these can significantly affect fish behavior.

10. Exercise Patience and Persistence:

River fishing requires patience and persistence. Not every fishing trip will result in the catch of a lifetime. However, remaining patient and persistent will eventually yield positive outcomes. Stay focused, observe the water, adjust your techniques, and keep casting in different areas until you find success. Remember, river fishing is an ever-changing environment, and each fishing trip provides an opportunity to learn and improve your skills.

In this chapter, we have explored a range of tricks and techniques that will significantly enhance your chances of river fishing success. From getting to know the river and understanding fish behavior to employing the right bait and mastering casting techniques, these tricks will equip you with the knowledge needed to tackle any river fishing adventure. Remember, the key to becoming a successful river angler lies in practice, observation, and perseverance. So grab your gear, head to the nearest river, and embark on an exciting fishing journey that promises unforgettable moments and memorable catches!

Tackling Challenges in Lake Fishing

Lake fishing has long been a popular pastime for anglers seeking tranquility in nature and the thrill of catching fish. However, unlike fishing in rivers or oceans, lake fishing comes with its own set of unique challenges. From navigating the vast expanse of water to understanding the behavior of fish, tackling these challenges requires knowledge, skill, and adaptability. In this chapter, we explore some of the key obstacles faced by lake anglers and offer valuable insights and practical tips to overcome them.

Navigating the Uncharted Waters:

One of the most significant challenges in lake fishing is navigating the seemingly endless expanse of water. Unlike rivers or smaller bodies of water, lakes can extend for miles, posing a constant dilemma for anglers. Unfamiliarity with the lake's layout can result in wasted time and frustration. To tackle this challenge, it is crucial to gather information about the lake before heading out.

Researching the lake's topography, hotspots, and even weather patterns can provide a valuable advantage. Consulting local maps, studying satellite imagery, and even talking to fellow anglers or local authorities can help in understanding the lake's structure. Some modern advancements, such as fish finders and GPS devices, also aid in navigating and locating fish in unfamiliar waters.

Understanding Fish Behavior:

Another challenge in lake fishing is comprehending the behavior of the underwater inhabitants, which can vary greatly depending on the species and their environment. Fish in lakes tend to have different feeding patterns than those found in rivers or oceans, making it necessary for anglers to adapt their strategies accordingly.

When fishing in lakes, it is important to understand the structure and the habitat preferences of different species. This knowledge can guide anglers in choosing the right fishing techniques, bait, and locations. For instance, largemouth bass are often found near underwater structures, such as fallen trees or submerged rocks. On the other hand, trout might be attracted to cooler, deeper waters with suitable cover.

Seasonal Variations:

Seasonal changes significantly impact fish behavior, making it crucial for lake anglers to adapt their approach accordingly. During warmer months, fish tend to seek cooler areas of the lake, deeper depths, or shaded spots where they can find respite from the heat. Moreover, aquatic vegetation blooms in the summer, providing cover and attracting various species.

In contrast, during colder months, fish tend to become less active and migrate towards warmer waters. Understanding these seasonal variations is essential in determining the best time to fish on a particular lake. This knowledge can positively influence bait selection, fishing techniques, and even the time of day to increase the likelihood of a successful catch.

Bait Selection and Presentation:

Selecting the right bait can be the difference between a rewarding fishing experience and returning empty-handed. Lake fishing presents a broad range of bait options, each suited to different fish species and situations. Understanding the behavior and feeding patterns of the target fish is crucial in choosing the correct bait.

Live bait, such as worms, minnows, or insects, often prove successful for a wide variety of species. Artificial baits, such as lures or flies, can also be effective, especially when mimicking the natural prey of the target fish. The color, size, and action of the bait are also important considerations, as they can influence the fish's reaction. Experimenting with different bait types and presentations is necessary to find what works best for a specific lake and target fish.

Patience and Persistence:

Lake fishing can test an angler's patience and persistence. Unlike rivers, where fish are often more active and opportunistic due to the constant flow of water and food, lakes can be more unpredictable. Fish may become increasingly selective or less inclined to feed, making it essential for anglers to exercise patience and remain persistent.

When fishing in lakes, it is advisable to spend an ample amount of time in one location before moving on to another. Fish often follow feeding patterns and may not be present in abundance throughout the entire lake. Spending a significant amount of time in an area increases the chances of encountering fish and learning their behavior.

Weather Factors:

Lake fishing is undoubtedly influenced by weather conditions, which can either work in favor of anglers or act as a significant challenge. Various weather factors, such as wind, temperature, and sunlight intensity, play a significant role in the feeding patterns and habitats of fish.

Wind, for instance, can create favorable conditions by causing waves that dislodge insects and other food into the water, thus attracting fish. On the other hand, strong winds can make maneuvering a boat difficult and influence casting accuracy. Monitoring weather forecasts and considering how the conditions may affect fish behavior can be helpful in planning a successful fishing trip.

Lake fishing offers a world of challenges that require anglers to adapt their skills, techniques, and strategies. From navigating vast waters to understanding fish behavior, tackling these hurdles can be both exciting and demanding. By gathering information, studying the lake's topography, and learning about the target species, anglers can increase their chances of a rewarding fishing experience. Patience, persistence, and a willingness to adapt to changing conditions are essential virtues that will contribute to success on the water. So next time you venture out onto the tranquil surface of a lake, be prepared to embrace the challenges and enjoy the thrill of the chase.

Adapting to Tides in Saltwater Fishing

The ebb and flow of the tides play a vital role in the world of saltwater fishing. Understanding and adapting to these tidal movements can significantly increase your chances of success on your angling expeditions. In this chapter, we will explore the intricacies of tidal patterns, their influence on fish behavior, and the various techniques and strategies you can employ to make the most of different tide conditions. So grab your fishing gear, and let's dive into the fascinating world of adapting to tides in saltwater fishing!

Understanding Tides:

Before we delve into the practical aspects of saltwater fishing, let's first understand the science behind tides. Tides are the periodic rise and fall of sea levels caused by the gravitational forces exerted by the moon and the sun on Earth's oceans. The intensity and movement of tides can vary depending on the location, shape of the coastline, and the alignment of the sun, moon, and Earth.

Tidal Movements and Fish Behavior:

Tidal movements have a profound impact on the behavior of marine life, including fish. Understanding how fish respond to these changes is crucial for anglers. Fish, particularly predatory species, often use tides as a cue for feeding. During high tides, water levels rise and inundate the marshes, flats, and other shallow areas, providing easy access to food sources like baitfish, crabs, and shrimp. On the other hand, during low tides, these prey species often concentrate and become trapped in smaller pools or channels, making them vulnerable to predatory fish.

Targeting Different Fish Species:

Now that we appreciate the link between tides and fish behavior, let's explore how you can adapt your saltwater fishing techniques to target specific species based on tidal phases.

1. High Tide Fishing:

During high tide, predatory fish often venture closer to the shorelines, mangroves, and flats, following the rising water to exploit the abundant food sources. To capitalize on this opportunity, consider using topwater lures, such as poppers or surface plugs. These lures mimic injured or struggling baitfish and can entice predatory fish like snook and redfish to strike aggressively. Casting around marshes, docks, oyster beds, and grassy areas close to the shore might yield excellent results.

2. Low Tide Fishing:

When the tide recedes, predatory fish often move to deeper channels, holes, or drop-offs where they can ambush prey as the water drains out. In such situations, deepwater fishing techniques like bottom fishing, jigging, or using live bait near these structures can effectively target species like flounder, trout, or grouper. Focus on casting your bait near underwater structures, such as submerged rocks, reefs, or wrecks, as these areas act as hiding spots for hungry fish during low tide.

3. Moving Tides:

The transition period between high and low tide, known as moving tides or tide changes, can be incredibly productive for anglers. The shifting water levels during these times stir up baitfish and other prey, creating feeding opportunities for a variety of fish species. During moving tides, consider using lures that mimic baitfish or present a realistic presentation. Techniques such as fishing with suspended jerkbaits, soft plastics, or suspending twitch baits can entice strikes from fish actively feeding during these tidal shifts.

Adapting Your Techniques:

While understanding the ideal fishing techniques for specific tidal conditions is crucial, there are also various other adaptations you can make to maximize your success in saltwater fishing.

1. Adjusting Retrieve Speed:

Modifying your retrieve speed can be an efficient technique when fishing in changing tidal conditions. During high tide or moving tides, fish tend to be more active and aggressive. In such scenarios, a fast and erratic retrieve might be more effective in triggering strikes.

Conversely, during low tide or when fish are not as active, a slower and more methodical retrieve might be necessary to entice reluctant feeders.

2. Identifying Current Breaks:

Current breaks are areas where the water flow is disrupted, providing a haven for fish seeking shelter, saving energy, or ambushing prey. These breaks can be caused by natural structures such as rock piles, jetties, or points, or even man-made structures like bridges or piers. Identifying and targeting these current breaks during different tidal phases can significantly increase your chances of success. Casting your bait or lure near these structures and allowing it to drift naturally with the current can be a highly effective strategy.

3. Utilizing Electronics:

With advancements in technology, today's anglers have an array of fish-finding equipment at their disposal. Take advantage of fish finders, depth sounders, and GPS devices to locate productive areas. By identifying drop-offs, ledges, or underwater structure using these tools, you can position yourself strategically, increasing your chances of landing a prized catch.

Adapting to tides in saltwater fishing is a skill that takes time and experience to develop. By understanding the principles behind tidal movements, comprehending fish behavior during different tide phases, and tailoring your techniques accordingly, you can significantly improve your success rate on the water. Remember, each tide brings its own set of challenges and opportunities, so embrace the ever-changing saltwater environment and approach every fishing trip as a chance to learn and adapt. Happy fishing!

Understanding Underwater Topography

1.1 The Hidden World Beneath the Waves

The vast majority of the Earth's surface is covered by water, and yet, it remains largely unexplored and full of mysteries waiting to be unraveled. One of the key aspects of this hidden world is underwater topography – the study of the physical features and landscapes that exist beneath the waves. Just as terrestrial topography helps us understand the landforms on Earth, underwater topography allows us to comprehend the mesmerizing beauty and complexity of the underwater realm.

1.2 The Importance of Underwater Topography

Underwater topography holds immense significance for various scientific disciplines, maritime navigation, and environmental conservation. Understanding the layout of the seafloor provides valuable insights into the geological processes shaping our planet, such as plate tectonics, erosion, and sedimentation. Moreover, knowledge of underwater topography aids in mapping underwater geological hazards, locating potential mineral resources, and planning infrastructure installations like undersea cables or pipelines.

1.3 Tools for Mapping Underwater Topography

Mapping the seafloor is an intricate task that requires a combination of cutting-edge technologies and age-old techniques. Sonar systems are widely used to scan the ocean floor using sound waves, producing detailed bathymetric maps. Multibeam sonar systems, in particular, offer enhanced precision, capturing multiple data points simultaneously and providing three-dimensional representations of underwater topography. Satellite imagery, gravity measurements, and laser scanning are also employed to complement sonar data, enabling scientists to create comprehensive maps that reveal the hidden features of the seafloor.

Chapter 2: Unveiling the Underwater Landscapes

2.1 Continental Shelves and Continental Slopes

As we embark on our journey to understand underwater topography, we encounter the first significant feature – continental shelves. These submerged extensions of the continents are typically shallow and gently sloping, leading up to the abrupt drop-off known as the continental slope. Continental shelves are havens for diverse marine life due to their ample sunlight penetration and nutrient-rich waters. The steep continental slope marks the beginning of the vast abyssal plains that dominate the deep ocean.

2.2 Abyssal Plains and Mid-Ocean Ridges

Abyssal plains comprise the largest continuous expanses of the seafloor, stretching across thousands of kilometers. These relatively flat regions are covered with fine sediment, accumulated over millions of years, carried by rivers or transported by ocean currents. Mid-ocean ridges, on the other hand, are the epicenters of tectonic activity. These underwater mountain ranges stretch for thousands of kilometers and are formed by the upwelling of magma from the Earth's mantle. The ridges act as boundaries between tectonic plates, fostering the creation of new crust and shaping the Earth's geological history.

2.3 Trenches and Submarine Canyons

While exploring underwater topography, we must not overlook some of the most dramatic features – trenches and submarine canyons. Trenches are the deepest parts of the seafloor, plunging several kilometers below the surface. These geologically active regions are often situated near subduction zones, where one tectonic plate is forced beneath another, giving rise to volcanic activity and violent earthquakes. Submarine canyons, on the other hand, are narrow, steep-sided valleys that cut through the continental shelves and slopes. These canyons are often formed by the erosive power of turbidity currents, underwater avalanches created by sediment-laden currents.

Chapter 3: Implications for Marine Life

3.1 Coral Reefs: Oases of Biodiversity

Underwater topography plays a crucial role in shaping marine ecosystems, most notably through the formation of coral reefs. Coral reefs are marine structures formed over thousands of years by the accumulation and growth of tiny coral polyps, which build intricate skeletons of calcium carbonate. These underwater marvels provide shelter and sustenance to a staggering array of marine species, making them one of the most biodiverse habitats on Earth. Understanding the topography of coral reefs allows scientists to better comprehend their distribution, growth patterns, and vulnerability to environmental changes.

3.2 Ocean Currents and Upwelling Zones

The intricate patterns of underwater topography significantly influence ocean circulation and the transport of heat, nutrients, and biological matter. Upwelling zones, areas where deep, nutrient-rich waters rise to the surface, are often associated with underwater topographic features such as seamounts or canyons. These zones stimulate the growth of phytoplankton and support the proliferation of diverse marine life, attracting large migratory species like whales and tuna.

Chapter 4: Navigating the Depths

4.1 Underwater Topography for Navigation and Exploration

Accurate knowledge of underwater topography is vital for safe navigation and exploration of the seas. Navigational charts, derived from detailed underwater topographic maps, allow mariners to steer clear of hazards like submerged rocks, reefs, or shipwrecks. Additionally, underwater topography aids in the determination of safe anchorage areas and the planning of maritime routes, ensuring efficient and secure passage for ships across the globe.

4.2 Underwater Archaeology

Underwater topography also plays a role in uncovering the secrets of our past, through the field of underwater archaeology. Shipwrecks and submerged archaeological sites provide invaluable insights into ancient civilizations, maritime history, and cultural heritage. Understanding the topography of these submerged landscapes helps experts map and identify potential locations of historical significance, allowing us to piece together stories that would otherwise remain lost to time.

Chapter 5: Future Perspectives and Environmental Conservation

5.1 Underwater Topography and Climate Change

As our understanding of underwater topography evolves, it becomes an essential tool in assessing and mitigating the impacts of climate change. Rising sea levels and changing ocean currents necessitate accurate bathymetric data to understand the potential risks to coastal regions, predict storm surges, and plan for sustainable coastal development. Moreover, underwater topography aids in the monitoring of the health of marine ecosystems, providing insights into the impacts of rising temperatures, ocean acidification, and other climate-related stressors.

5.2 Preserving Underwater Heritage

Recognizing the significance of underwater topography introduces the importance of preserving these fragile and valuable ecosystems. Marine protected areas, established based on detailed knowledge of seafloor landscapes, help safeguard biodiversity, prevent destructive practices like trawling, and promote responsible marine resource management. Conservation efforts involving underwater topography are instrumental in ensuring that future generations can explore and appreciate the wonders of the underwater world.

Chapter 8: Safety and Preparedness

Fishing is an enjoyable and rewarding activity that allows people to connect with nature and pursue their passion for angling. However, it is crucial to prioritize safety when engaging in any outdoor activity, especially fishing. The seventh chapter of our book discussed the different fishing techniques and equipment, helping you choose the right gear for your fishing expeditions. In this chapter, we will explore the essential aspects of safety and preparedness for fishing, providing you with the knowledge and tools necessary to ensure your well-being during your angling adventures.

Understanding the Environment:

Before venturing out for a fishing trip, it is crucial to have a comprehensive understanding of the environment in which you will be fishing. Study the water body – whether it's a river, lake, or the ocean – and familiarize yourself with potential hazards, such as strong currents, sharp rocks, or submerged debris. Taking note of any potential dangers will allow you to prepare adequately and take necessary precautions to mitigate risks.

Checking Weather Conditions:

Weather conditions can have a significant impact on the safety of a fishing trip. Before heading out, it is essential to check the weather forecast for your intended fishing location. Keep in mind that sudden weather changes can occur, so it's wise to have a portable weather radio or a smartphone with a reliable weather app to stay updated. In case of severe weather warnings, it is advisable to postpone your fishing plans to another day.

Essential Safety Equipment:

No fishing trip is complete without essential safety equipment. It's crucial to have a well-stocked first aid kit, including items such as bandages, antiseptic ointments, tweezers, and any necessary personal medications. Additionally, a properly fitting life jacket for each person on board is an absolute must when fishing from a boat. Even experienced swimmers can benefit from wearing a life jacket, as accidents can happen quickly and unexpectedly. Apart from life jackets, other recommended safety equipment includes a throwable flotation device, a whistle, and a signaling mirror.

Boat Safety Precautions:

For those planning to fish from a boat, it is important to follow certain safety precautions. Ensure that the boat is in good working condition, examining the engine, steering, and hull. Verify that all required safety equipment, such as the life jackets, throwable flotation device, fire extinguisher, and navigation lights, are present and functional. Familiarize yourself with the boat's capacity limits and only invite enough anglers to adhere to these limits. Furthermore, always inform someone trustworthy about your fishing plans, including your destination and expected return time, so they can contact the authorities if needed.

Fishing with Others:

While fishing can be a solitary endeavor, having a fishing buddy is not only more enjoyable but also significantly safer. Fishing with a partner increases the likelihood of swift assistance in case of an emergency. In challenging or unfamiliar fishing locations, two heads are undoubtedly better than one. Additionally, sharing knowledge and experience with a fellow angler can enhance your overall fishing skills and increase your chances of success.

Casting Safety:

Casting is an integral part of fishing, but it can also be potentially dangerous if not practiced with care. Always make sure there is no one within your casting range, both on the boat and onshore. Notify your fishing partner before casting and agree on a safe distance between yourself and others. Be aware of any low-hanging trees or branches that could snag your fishing line during your cast, potentially causing injury or damaging your equipment.

Wading Safety:

Wading in rivers or streams while fishing can provide access to prime fishing spots, but it also poses additional safety considerations. Always wear suitable wading boots or shoes with good traction to prevent slipping on wet rocks or surfaces. Use a wading staff or a sturdy stick to maintain balance, especially when navigating through strong currents. Take caution while crossing deeper areas and be familiar with the river's flow and depth before attempting to wade through it. It is advisable to use a wading belt to prevent water from filling your waders in case of a fall.

Anchoring and Mooring:

When fishing from a boat, proper anchoring or mooring techniques are crucial to ensure your safety. Understand the specific requirements and techniques for anchoring or mooring based on the water body you are fishing in. Ensure that the anchor or mooring lines are in good condition and not frayed or weakened. Use a suitable anchor or mooring system according to the size and weight of your boat, as an inadequate system may not hold the boat securely and can lead to unnecessary risks.

Dealing with Emergencies:

Despite taking all necessary precautions, emergencies can still occur while fishing. Therefore, it is essential to be prepared and know how to handle different emergency situations. In case of a severe injury, immediately administer first aid and call for professional help if needed. Keep a fully charged cell phone or a marine radio onboard to contact emergency services in case of an emergency or to provide your location in case you need assistance. Additionally, understanding basic navigation skills and carrying a compass or GPS can be invaluable if you get disoriented or lost.

Safety and preparedness are paramount when it comes to fishing. By understanding the environment, checking weather conditions, having the right safety equipment, following boat safety precautions, fishing with others, practicing casting and wading safety, and knowing how to handle emergencies, you can ensure a safe and enjoyable fishing experience. Always remember that being well-prepared and vigilant contributes to your personal well-being and the well-being of those around you. Stay safe and happy fishing!

Weather Wisdom and Its Significance

Fishing is an ancient practice that has served as a vital source of sustenance and livelihood for countless communities across the globe. Throughout history, fishermen have relied on their knowledge of weather patterns and their understanding of the intricacies of nature in order to maximize their chances of a successful catch. Weather wisdom, acquired through observation and experience, has become an essential tool in the fisherman's arsenal.

Chapter 1: The Foundations of Weather Wisdom

1.1 Observing Nature's Clues

In ancient times, fishermen had no sophisticated weather prediction tools, such as barometers or satellites. Instead, they turned to nature to forecast impending weather changes. By observing animals, plants, clouds, and winds, they could discern patterns and make informed decisions about their fishing expeditions.

1.2 Animals as Weather Indicators

Animals often possess an uncanny ability to sense changes in atmospheric conditions, behaving accordingly. For example, seagulls flying inland or cows lying down indicate the approach of a storm, while birds singing more loudly than usual can signal an approaching weather change. Understanding these natural cues allows fishermen to prepare for inclement weather or choose the best time and place for fishing.

1.3 Clouds and Wind

Cloud formations and wind patterns provide valuable information about forthcoming weather conditions. For example, cirrus clouds often precede a warm front and indicate a possible improvement in fishing conditions. Understanding the different types of clouds and their implications can help fishermen anticipate rainfall, storms, or clear skies, allowing them to adjust their strategies accordingly.

Chapter 2: The Science Behind Weather Patterns

2.1 Atmospheric Pressure

The pressure exerted by the atmosphere plays a crucial role in predicting weather changes. A sudden drop in atmospheric pressure usually signifies the approach of a storm, while a rise in pressure suggests fair weather. By tracking these changes through barometric readings, fishermen can gauge the upcoming conditions and adjust their fishing plans accordingly.

2.2 Wind Direction and Speed

Wind is another critical element influencing fishing conditions. Understanding the correlation between wind direction and fish behavior helps fishermen predict where fish might be congregating. For instance, an onshore breeze often brings baitfish closer to shore, attracting larger predator fish. Monitoring wind speed is also essential, as strong gusts can disrupt feeding patterns and make fishing difficult.

Chapter 3: Utilizing Weather Wisdom for Successful Fishing

3.1 Choosing the Right Time

Leveraging weather wisdom enables fishermen to determine the most favorable times for casting their lines. Calm conditions and stable atmospheric pressure are usually optimal for fishing, as they create a sense of stability and tranquility in aquatic environments. Pausing during periods of unstable weather, such as storms or rapidly changing atmospheric pressure, can provide fishermen with an opportunity to reinforce their knowledge of local weather patterns.

3.2 Identifying Fish Behavior

Weather patterns affect fish behavior, and astute fishermen can discern these nuances to their advantage. For example, barometric pressure changes influence fish buoyancy, leading them to travel at different depths. By tracking pressure fluctuations, fishermen can adjust bait and tackle placements accordingly, improving their chances of hooking a catch.

3.3 Adapting Techniques

When faced with specific weather conditions, successful fishermen adapt their fishing techniques accordingly. For instance, low light conditions, such as overcast skies or sunrise/sunset periods, often trigger heightened fish activity near the water's surface. Adjusting bait depth, using different lure colors or patterns, or modifying retrieval speeds can improve the likelihood of attracting fish during these times.

Chapter 4: The Role of Technology in Weather Wisdom

4.1 Modern Tools and Forecasts

Advancements in technology have revolutionized weather prediction and forecasting, providing fishermen with more accurate and timely information. Access to real-time weather data, satellite imagery, and specialized weather apps empower anglers to make informed decisions about their fishing trips. Paired with traditional weather wisdom, modern tools enhance the ability to maximize fishing opportunities.

4.2 GPS and Navigation

Global Positioning System (GPS) technology has simplified navigation for fishermen, allowing them to identify and mark productive fishing spots with precision. Additionally, GPS-enabled devices can provide location-specific weather updates, helping anglers avoid hazardous weather conditions or identify ideal fishing windows.

Weather wisdom is a valuable asset for any fisherman, offering insights into the ever-changing dynamics of the natural world. From observing animal behavior to analyzing cloud formations and using modern technology, understanding weather patterns enhances the chances of a successful fishing expedition. By combining ancient wisdom with modern science, fishermen can continue to harness the power of the elements and increase their opportunities for a bountiful catch.

Essential Gear for Personal Safety

Fishing is a popular and enjoyable pastime that allows people to connect with nature, spend time in serene surroundings, and even catch their own dinner. However, amidst the excitement and relaxation, it's important not to overlook the significance of personal safety. While fishing may seem like a harmless activity, it can come with its own set of risks and challenges. In this chapter, we will explore the essential gear needed to ensure your personal safety while fishing, including life jackets, wading belts, protective clothing, footwear, and personal floatation devices.

Life Jackets:

One of the most critical pieces of gear when it comes to personal safety during fishing is a life jacket or personal flotation device (PFD). It is important to remember that accidents can happen even to the most experienced anglers, and unexpectedly finding oneself in deep water can be life-threatening. A properly fitting life jacket is designed to keep you afloat until help arrives or until you can swim to safety. It is crucial to choose a PFD that is specifically designed for fishing and offers both comfort and functionality. Look for a life jacket with adjustable straps, multiple storage pockets, and high visibility colors. Ensure that the life jacket is US Coast Guard-approved and suitable for your body weight and size.

Wading Belts:

For those who enjoy wading while fishing, a wading belt is an essential piece of safety gear. Wading in rivers, streams, or other bodies of water can be treacherous due to slippery rocks and strong currents. By wearing a wading belt, you can prevent water from entering your waders in the event of a fall. This helps to reduce the risk of being dragged down by heavy, water-filled waders, which can compromise your ability to swim and ultimately put your life in danger. Ensure that your wading belt is made of high-quality materials and properly adjust it to achieve a snug fit around your waist before entering the water.

Protective Clothing:

When it comes to personal safety during fishing, protective clothing plays a significant role in safeguarding yourself from the elements and potential injuries. Choose clothing that provides protection from harmful sun UV rays, mosquitoes, insects, and other biting pests. A wide-brimmed hat can shield your face and neck from the sun, reducing the risk of sunburn or heatstroke. Long-sleeved shirts, made from lightweight and breathable fabric, can provide additional protection while keeping you cool. It is also essential to wear gloves to prevent abrasions, cuts, or punctures when handling fish or other sharp objects associated with fishing.

Footwear:

Selecting the appropriate footwear is crucial for maintaining personal safety while fishing. Slippery rocks, algae-covered surfaces, or muddy terrains can pose severe injury risks if you don't have proper traction. When choosing fishing footwear, opt for sturdy, non-slip soles that offer excellent grip. Depending on your fishing location and preferences, you can choose between wading boots, fishing sandals, or water shoes. It's essential to ensure that your footwear is comfortable and adequately supports your feet, ankles, and arches, reducing the risk of sprains or twists while moving across uneven terrain.

Personal Floatation Devices:

In addition to life jackets, personal floatation devices (PFDs) designed specifically for fishing are available as an added safety measure. These devices provide flotation support while allowing anglers greater freedom of movement for casting, reeling, and netting fish. PFDs typically feature multiple adjustable straps, D-rings for attaching gear, and often have pockets for storing small accessories. These devices are lightweight and can be worn comfortably for extended fishing periods. Rather than replacing a traditional life jacket, personal floatation devices act as a supplemental safety measure for anglers who prefer to remain mobile and agile while on the water.

Emergency Whistle and Signaling Devices:

When fishing in remote locations or areas with limited visibility, it's crucial to have signaling devices to attract attention in case of an emergency. An emergency whistle is a compact and effective tool for alerting nearby individuals or search parties of your presence. Additionally, consider carrying a signaling mirror, flares, or a waterproof strobe light to attract attention from a distance. Always familiarize yourself with the proper use of these signaling devices and remember to pack them in a waterproof container to prevent damage or loss due to exposure to water.

In this chapter, we have explored the essential gear for personal safety while fishing. Life jackets, wading belts, protective clothing, footwear, personal floatation devices, emergency whistles, and signaling devices are just some of the equipment that should be considered when engaging in this beloved pastime. By being proactive and prepared with the right gear, anglers can mitigate risks, increase their personal safety, and focus on enjoying the wonders of fishing. Whether you're a seasoned angler or just starting out, personal safety should always remain a top priority, allowing you to fully appreciate the joys of fishing in a secure and worry-free manner.

Emergency Protocols and First Aid

Fishing is a delightful and rejuvenating hobby that allows individuals to unwind and connect with nature. However, just like any outdoor activity, it comes with its fair share of risks. Accidents can happen, and being prepared for emergencies is crucial to ensure the safety of all anglers. In this chapter, we will discuss the fundamental emergency protocols and first aid techniques specifically tailored to those venturing into the world of fishing.

Assessing the Situation

In any emergency, the ability to assess the situation swiftly and correctly is paramount. Whether you are fishing on a boat, dock, or riverbank, always remain alert and observant of your surroundings. Identifying potential dangers, such as treacherous terrain or unpredictable weather, can prevent accidents from occurring and allow you to react promptly if an incident does happen.

Furthermore, it is imperative to be knowledgeable about the specific fishing location. Knowing the nearest emergency services, medical facilities, or even the contact details of other anglers nearby can significantly expedite response time in case of an emergency. Additionally, having a reliable means of communication, such as a fully charged mobile phone or two-way radio, can be a lifesaver in critical situations.

Common Fishing Accidents

While fishing accidents can vary widely, some common incidents occur more frequently than others. By being familiar with these mishaps, anglers can better prepare themselves for potential emergencies. Here are some of the most common fishing accidents and how to handle them:

1. Hook Injuries: Accidents involving hooks are quite common in fishing. If you or a fellow angler gets hooked, avoid removing the hook forcefully, as it can result in further injury. Instead, assess the situation and consider two options: either cut the barbless hook near the skin and push it through, or seek medical assistance for hook removal if necessary.

2. Falls and Slips: Fishing often involves navigating uneven terrain, both on land and boats. Accidental slips and falls can result in injuries ranging from minor bruises to broken bones. In the event of a fall, first ensure everyone's safety and assess the severity of the injury. Administer first aid accordingly and seek professional medical help if needed.

3. Strains and Sprains: Overexertion or incorrect handling of fishing equipment can lead to muscle strains or sprains. Proper warm-up exercises, correct lifting techniques, and using appropriate gear can minimize the risk of such injuries. In case of a strain or sprain, practice the R.I.C.E. method: Rest, Ice, Compression, and Elevation.

First Aid Techniques for Fishing Emergencies

Prompt and effective first aid in fishing emergencies can make a significant difference in the outcome. While it is crucial to receive comprehensive first aid training, here are some fundamental techniques to remember:

1. Stabilizing Fractures and Dislocations: In the unfortunate event of a fracture or dislocation during fishing, immobilization is key. Use available resources, such as splints, blankets, or clothing, to stabilize the injured area before seeking professional medical help.

2. Controlling Bleeding: Fishing accidents can cause bleeding, ranging from minor cuts to more severe wounds. To control bleeding, apply direct pressure on the wound using a clean cloth or bandage. Elevating the injured area often helps reduce blood flow. If bleeding is severe or does not stop, call for emergency medical assistance.

3. Treating Burns: Fishing often involves open fires, camp stoves, and hot cooking equipment. In the case of burns, promptly cool the affected area under running water for at least 20 minutes. Cover the burn with a sterile dressing or clean cloth to prevent infection and seek medical attention if necessary.

4. Hypothermia and Heat Exhaustion: Being exposed to extreme temperatures can lead to hypothermia or heat exhaustion. Recognizing the signs, such as shivering, confusion, or excessive

sweating, is vital. Treat hypothermia by gradually warming the person using warm blankets and fluids. For heat exhaustion, move the individual to a cool place, elevate their legs, and provide them with plenty of water.

In the world of fishing, emergencies can arise unexpectedly. By being well-prepared and equipped with the knowledge of emergency protocols and first aid techniques, anglers can ensure their safety and that of their fellow fishing enthusiasts. Remember, these guidelines are not exhaustive, and it is essential to receive proper first aid training. Always prioritize safety, assess risks, and be vigilant in order to enjoy this wonderful hobby to its fullest extent. Happy fishing and stay safe!

Staying Mindful in Outdoor Environments

When it comes to fishing, it's not just about casting your line and reeling in a big catch. It's an experience that allows us to immerse ourselves in the beauty of nature, escape the daily grind, and find solace in the outdoors. However, to fully appreciate this unique activity, it is crucial to stay mindful and attuned to your surroundings. In this chapter, we will explore the concept of mindfulness in outdoor environments for fishing and discover the various ways it enhances our overall fishing experience.

The Essence of Mindfulness:

Mindfulness is more than just a trendy buzzword; it's a way of living fully in the present moment. When it comes to fishing, staying mindful involves engaging your senses and being aware of the intricate details of your surroundings. It means breathing in the crisp morning air, feeling the gentle caress of the breeze on your skin, and immersing yourself in the symphony of natural sounds. By staying mindful, we open ourselves up to a richer and more fulfilling fishing experience.

Experiencing Nature:

When we engage with the great outdoors, it's important to be fully present and appreciate the wonders of Mother Nature. Whether you're standing on the bank of a serene lake, wading in a rushing river, or casting your line into the vastness of the ocean, staying mindful allows you to establish a deep connection with your environment. Each outdoor location has its unique appeal, and by being present, you can fully immerse yourself in the beauty that surrounds you.

Take a moment to observe the colors of the landscape, the dance of the sunlight on the water's surface, and the myriad of plant and animal life coexisting harmoniously. Be aware of the gentle rustling of leaves, the distant calls of birds, and the soothing sound of water flowing. These simple pleasures are often overlooked, but they can elevate your fishing experience from mere recreation to a spiritual communion with nature.

Appreciating the Details:

Part of being mindful in outdoor environments for fishing is taking notice of the small and often overlooked elements that make up the bigger picture. Mindfulness encourages us to appreciate the intricate details, such as the delicate patterns on a butterfly's wings or the vibrant colors of a dragonfly perched on a lily pad. By staying mindful, we can marvel at the delicate ecosystem that supports the fish we seek, understanding that each element plays a vital role.

Additionally, paying attention to the surrounding flora can provide valuable insights for a successful fishing expedition. Observing the blossoming of certain plants can signal the presence of specific insects, which, in turn, can attract fish. Being mindful of these details can significantly improve your chances of a fruitful day on the water.

Safety and Mindfulness:

While the allure of nature's beauty is captivating, it's essential to remember that outdoor environments bring with them certain risks. Staying mindful encompasses being aware of potential dangers and taking necessary precautions to ensure your safety and the safety of those around you.

Before embarking on a fishing excursion, it's crucial to familiarize yourself with the area's rules and regulations. This helps protect vulnerable ecosystems and ensures a sustainable fishing experience for generations to come. Additionally, being mindful of weather conditions and checking for potential hazards like strong currents, slippery terrain, or nearby wildlife can help you navigate safely through your fishing journey.

Conservation and Ethical Fishing:

As responsible anglers, it is our duty to practice ethical fishing and protect the delicate balance of the ecosystems we enjoy. Mindfulness plays a significant role in promoting sustainable fishing practices and supporting conservation efforts.

Mindfulness involves being aware of catch limits, adhering to size restrictions, and practicing catch-and-release whenever possible. By respecting these regulations, we ensure the long-term viability of fish populations and contribute to the preservation of our favorite fishing spots. Remember, as stewards of nature, our actions have a direct impact on the health of aquatic habitats and the fish that inhabit them.

Cultivating Mindfulness Through Fishing Techniques:

Fishing techniques themselves can serve as a gateway to mindfulness. By engaging in activities like fly fishing, for example, one can fully immerse themselves in the present moment. The rhythmic casting of the line and the fluid dance between angler and water create a harmonious connection that transcends the mere act of catching fish. Fly fishing, in particular, encourages an acute awareness of the environment, requires precision and patience, and ultimately fosters a deep appreciation for the process rather than the outcome.

Staying mindful in outdoor environments for fishing is more than a passing trend; it's a transformational experience that allows us to connect with nature on a deeper level. By immersing ourselves in the wonders of the natural world, observing the intricate details, and practicing ethical fishing, we can enhance our fishing journeys. Remember, fishing is not just about catching fish; it's about embracing the beauty around you, appreciating the delicate ecosystems that sustain us, and fostering a sense of unity with the environment. So next time you head out to cast your line, take a moment to slow down, breathe, and allow yourself to be fully present in the natural wonder that awaits you.

Chapter 9: Tales from Seasoned Anglers

In the vast world of fishing, few experiences compare to the wisdom and expertise gained by seasoned anglers. These individuals have dedicated countless hours to perfecting their craft, exploring hidden fishing spots, and amassing a treasure trove of unforgettable stories. Chapter 9 delves into the captivating tales and invaluable insights shared by these experienced individuals who have cast their lines far and wide. Through their adventures and misadventures, we discover the essence of the angling spirit and the deep connection between man and nature.

The Mysterious Tale of Old Joe's Secret Spot:

Deep in the heart of the Louisiana bayous, hidden amongst the dense vegetation, lies a secret spot known only to a select few – Old Joe's Honey Hole. Rumors of this mythical fishing haven have circulated for decades, its location whispered only among seasoned anglers. One evening, slumped over a weathered bar, Old Joe reluctantly revealed the tale behind the enigmatic waters.

According to the legend, as a young boy, Old Joe stumbled upon a small, winding creek while chasing after a wild hog. Despite his initial fears, he discovered a magical oasis brimming with life. The creek teemed with colossal bass and monstrous catfish that seemed to defy belief. Word of this paradise spread, yet few could locate it amid the tangled marshes and deceptive cypress trees.

As the years wore on, Old Joe became a master of navigation through these treacherous waters and acquired the uncanny ability to sniff out prime fishing grounds. His uncanny intuition allowed him to catch fish even on the foggiest mornings. Today, Old Joe holds the location of his secret spot close to his chest, passing it down only to his most trusted protégés, ensuring that the honey hole remains a testament to the pursuit of angling excellence.

The Timeless Battle with Moby Pike:

In the icy depths of Lake Superior, where winds whip across the rocky shores, lies an epic tale that has become legendary in angling circles. It is the tale of Moby Pike, a massive northern pike that haunts the dreams of seasoned anglers.

Captain J.D. Anderson, a seasoned fisherman with years of experience on the lake, regaled us with his fearsome encounter with this fierce predator. It was during the heart of winter when the icy stillness enveloped the lake, creating an eerie ambiance. J.D. set out in his trusty boat, determination etched across his face.

After hours of patience, his line suddenly jerked with an otherworldly force, nearly ripping him off his seat. Struggling with every ounce of strength, J.D. battled against Moby Pike, whose immense size was matched only by its ferocity. The struggle lasted for what felt like an eternity, the icy air biting at their faces. Eventually, the colossal creature broke free from the line, escaping back into the fathomless depths.

Despite losing the battle, J.D. returned home with a newfound resolve. He swore to fish Lake Superior until the day he could finally land Moby Pike, cementing his status not only as an experienced angler but also as a fearless warrior, relentlessly pursuing his prey.

Unveiling the Enigma of the Silver Shoal:

Roaming the windswept coasts of New Zealand, our chapter takes us to a place of solitude and timeless beauty - the Silver Shoal. This ethereal fishing spot, crafted by nature's hand, seems to exist on the edge of another world. Only those privileged enough to cast their lines here can fully understand its allure.

Within the confines of the Silver Shoal, legends are born and memories are etched into the souls of those who visit. Captain Sarah Evans, a seasoned angler who calls these mesmerizing waters her home, guides us through her favorite fishing experiences. In hushed tones, she speaks of shimmering schools of snapper, the gentle whisper of waves, and the tranquility shared between angler and fish.

Sarah recounts moments of intense struggle, when even the simplest catch demands extraordinary skill. Yet, she also reveals the inherent beauty of this spot, highlighting the importance of respecting the marine life that graces these azure waters.

Chapter 9 has uncovered the captivating tales and invaluable wisdom of seasoned anglers from around the world. From the mysteries of Old Joe's secret spot to the relentless pursuit of Moby Pike and the serenity of the Silver Shoal, the angling spirit shines brightly through their stories.

These seasoned anglers remind us of the timeless connection between man and nature, teaching us the importance of patience, perseverance, and stewardship. As we explore their tales, we are transported to distant waters and learn from their experiences, furthering our own appreciation for the world beneath the depths.

Legendary Catches and Near Misses

The sun was just beginning to peek over the horizon, casting a golden hue across the tranquil waters of Glass Lake. It was a cool, crisp morning, with a gentle breeze rustling the leaves on the surrounding trees. As the mist rolled softly across the surface of the water, a group of seasoned anglers gathered at the edge of the lake, their eyes filled with anticipation and excitement. These men and women had dedicated their lives to the pursuit of the perfect catch, an elusive prize that had become the stuff of legends. Today, they hoped to add their names to the annals of the greatest fishing stories ever told.

The art of fishing has always held a deep fascination for humans. From ancient civilizations to modern-day anglers, there is something inherently captivating about the chase, the unpredictability, and the triumph of outsmarting a creature from beneath the surface. It is a sport that demands patience, skill, and a keen understanding of the natural world. And, every now and then, it rewards these dedicated individuals with a moment of pure magic.

Throughout history, there have been countless legendary catches that have become the stuff of folklore. Tales of monstrous fish that tested the strength of men and their tackle, battling against the odds in a titanic struggle of wills. One such story is that of Captain James "Big Jim" Sullivan, a renowned angler from the northern coast of

Scotland. For years, Big Jim had been on the hunt for the fabled Loch Ness Monster, a creature rumored to lurk in the depths of the famous Scottish lake. Many had tried and failed to catch a glimpse of the elusive monster, but Big Jim was determined to succeed where others had faltered.

Armed with a state-of-the-art underwater camera and an impenetrable net, Big Jim set out on a foggy morning, navigating his boat through the mist-covered waters. Hours passed, and Big Jim's perseverance began to waver. But just when he was about to give up, he saw a massive ripple on the surface of the lake, followed by a protruding hump slowly emerging from the depths. It was the Loch Ness Monster itself.

With a surge of adrenaline, Big Jim quickly maneuvered his boat closer to the creature. In a daring move, he cast his net, hoping to capture the beast for further study. But the creature was faster and stronger than he could have ever imagined. It thrashed about wildly, sending waves crashing against the boat. Just as Big Jim thought he had succeeded in his mission, the net snapped under the sheer force of the monster's fury. The Loch Ness Monster vanished back into the depths, leaving Big Jim with nothing more than a broken net and an extraordinary tale to tell.

While some anglers pursue the thrill of reeling in a legendary catch, others find themselves on the precipice of a near-miss. These heart-stopping moments, when victory seems within grasp before being cruelly snatched away, are etched into the memories of those who experience them. One such tale of a near-miss takes us to the vast open seas, where brave anglers search for the mighty marlin.

Deep-sea fishing for marlin is an adrenaline-fueled pursuit that requires nerves of steel and unwavering determination. The ocean's vastness is both alluring and intimidating, with mysteries concealed beneath the surface that few will ever witness. Captain Rodrigo Martinez, a weathered seafarer hailing from the tropical shores of Costa Rica, had devoted his life to unlocking the secrets of the marlin's habitat.

One fateful day, Captain Martinez set out on his trusty vessel, armed with a custom-made rod and an abundance of hope. Hours turned into days as he scanned the horizon, searching for any signs of these majestic creatures. Then, on the fourth day of his expedition, a massive shadow appeared, racing towards his boat at an astonishing speed. It was a grander, the largest and most elusive of all marlins.

The battle that ensued was like nothing Captain Martinez had ever experienced. The marlin erupted from the ocean, its tail glistening spectacularly in the sunlight. With every twist and turn, the line strained, threatening to snap. The captain's muscles burned and his hands bled, but he refused to give up. Inch by inch, he fought to bring the marlin closer, to claim victory over this magnificent adversary.

Just as victory was in sight, a deafening snap shattered the silence. The rod splintered, unable to withstand the incredible force exerted by the marlin. Captain Martinez watched in disbelief as the creature disappeared beneath the waves, leaving him with nothing more than a broken rod and an epic tale of the one that got away.

Some may argue that it is not the catch itself, but the journey and the stories that emerge from these legendary catches and near-misses that truly capture the heart of fishing. They embody the essence of adventure, the thrill of the unknown, and the resilience of those who dare to tread in the realms of nature's playground. These stories, passed down through generations, serve as a testament to the human spirit, showcasing the indomitable will of those who strive to conquer the elements, one cast at a time.

So, as the anglers stood by the edge of Glass Lake, their eyes filled with dreams of conquering legendary catches and tales of near-misses, they knew that whatever the outcome, their passion for fishing would forever connect them to a rich tapestry of human history. For in the pursuit of the perfect catch, they had become part of something much larger than themselves—a timeless tradition woven into the very fabric of our existence.

Lessons Learned on the Waters

As the sun begins its ascent over the horizon, casting a golden glow across the tranquil waters, experienced anglers know that they are about to embark on a journey where Mother Nature reveals her secrets only to those who are patient, persistent, and well-prepared. In this chapter, we dive deep into the waters, exploring the invaluable lessons learned on countless fishing adventures - the triumphs, the failures, and the indelible wisdom gained along the way. Join me now as we cast off towards a treasure chest of experiences, uncovering the true essence of angling and discovering the delicate dance between man and fish.

Section 1: The Art of Patience

In the calm silence of a suspended line, patience becomes an art form, testing the resolve and fortitude of even the most seasoned angler. The teachings of the waters remind us that patience is far more than just waiting for a tug on our lines; it is an integral part of the angling experience that teaches us to appreciate the present moment. Whether awaiting the rise of a feeding fish or waiting for that elusive tug from a wily predator, the key lies in embracing the stillness and allowing our instincts to guide us.

Within the eternal tug-of-war between fate and dedication, we unravel the inherent connection between patience and perseverance. As we endure long hours of waiting, the myriad thoughts, hopes, and dreams that wander through our minds crystallize, reminding us not only of our commitment to the art but also of the importance of mental fortitude.

Section 2: Harnessing the Power of Persistence

Persistence is the weapon of choice when angling tests our determination. The art of fishing demands that we face and embrace the challenges bestowed upon us by the waters. It teaches us to keep casting, to resist the temptation to give up too soon, and to remain steadfast even in the face of discouragement. For every lost battle with the tides, our resilience strengthens, honing our skills as we strive for the ultimate accomplishment - the perfect catch.

Through countless trials and tribulations, we learn to adapt our tactics, experiment with different lures, and explore new techniques. Persistence molds us into agile and versatile anglers, never settling for mediocrity, and continuously seeking ways to improve. Every failed attempt becomes a valuable lesson etched upon our journey, inching us closer towards unraveling the enigma that is the natural world.

Section 3: The Multifaceted Art of Preparation

Preparation is the backbone of any successful fishing expedition. Superior knowledge of the waters, the nuances of different fish species, their habitats, and preferred feeding habits sets a well-prepared angler apart. The angling experience is akin to a grand puzzle wherein each detail and ounce of knowledge dovetails harmoniously.

From meticulously selecting the appropriate rods, reels, and lines to studying weather patterns and lunar cycles, every aspect of angling preparation contributes to the ultimate capture. We learn the value of local wisdom, consult experienced companions, and never underestimate the power of research. By equipping ourselves with an ocean of knowledge, we dare to push the boundaries of our previous experiences, delving deeper into realms that were once considered unattainable.

As we navigate the ebb and flow of the fishing world, the lessons learned on the waters become etched into our very being. Patience whispers its secrets, urging us to seek solace in the stillness of the present moment. Persistence infuses our spirits, encouraging us to cast again and again, never bowing to defeat. Preparation intertwines itself with our very essence, ensuring that we embark on every fishing expedition armed with the knowledge necessary to seize golden opportunities.

Each chapter of our angling endeavors unveils new insights and humbling experiences. From stretches of joyous triumphs to periods of humble introspection, we continue to grow as individuals, our bond with nature strengthening every step of the way. As the sun sets on this chapter, let us eagerly anticipate the next, as the lessons learned on the waters are boundless, and the journey itself is the truest reward an angler can receive.

Cultural and Historical Fishing Anecdotes

Throughout history, fishing has been an integral part of human culture. From providing sustenance to serving as a source of livelihood and entertainment, this age-old practice has left a profound impact on various civilizations. Each culture has its unique fishing traditions, accompanied by a plethora of captivating anecdotes that have been passed down through generations. In this chapter, we delve into the fascinating world of cultural and historical fishing anecdotes, exploring the stories that have shaped our perception of this timeless pursuit.

The Tale of Iktomi and the Sturgeon (Plains Tribes, North America)

Among the indigenous peoples of the Great Plains, fishing tales portray the cunning nature of Iktomi, the spider-trickster figure. In this particular story, Iktomi encounters a legendary sturgeon, known for its immense size and elusive nature. Determined to catch the prized fish, Iktomi crafts an intricate plan involving a handwoven net and an elaborate decoy. Despite his cunning, Iktomi's efforts are futile, as the sturgeon outwits him at every turn. This tale serves as a reminder that even the most cunning individuals can be humbled by the vast wisdom of nature.

The Samurai and the Golden Koi (Edo Period, Japan)

During the Edo period in Japan, fishing represented not only a means of sustenance but also a spiritual practice. The Samurai, known for their discipline and unwavering spirit, often sought serenity through the art of fishing. One particular tale tells of a samurai who embarked on a quest to catch the mythical golden koi. It was believed that encountering this radiant fish would bring immense luck and prosperity. Spending countless days by the tranquil pond, the samurai honed his fishing skills and eventually succeeded in capturing the elusive golden koi. This story highlights the harmony between man and nature and the rewards that come with patience and persistence.

The Mermaid's Song (Viking Era, Scandinavia)

In the mystical world of Norse mythology, fishing tales were often intertwined with legends of mermaids. It was said that mermaids possessed an enchanting voice capable of luring fishermen to their watery demise. One haunting tale recounts the encounter between a Viking fisherman and a mesmerizing mermaid. As the fisherman cast his net, he heard a melodic voice singing a hauntingly beautiful tune. Transfixed by the ethereal melody, the fisherman was drawn closer to the mermaid, unaware of the treacherous rocks that lay beneath the surface. Miraculously, he managed to escape just in the nick of time, forever entranced by the song that narrowly led to his downfall. This tale reflects the ancient belief in the mystical powers of the sea and the allure that mermaids held over the hearts of seafarers.

The Sacred Fishing Grounds (Incan Empire, South America)

In the vast Incan Empire, fishing was not merely a means of sustenance but a sacred ritual that symbolized the connection between man and the divine. One story tells of a revered elder who charted the sacred fishing grounds, ensuring that each village adhered to strict laws regarding the timing and location of their fishing expeditions. It was believed that these rules were set by the gods themselves, and any violation would result in dire consequences. The tale recounts a time when a village neglected the regulations and ventured into forbidden waters. The punishment was swift and severe, with a tremendous storm engulfing their fleet, casting all the fishermen into the wrathful sea. This tale serves as a reminder of the importance of respecting nature and adhering to age-old wisdom.

Shamans and the Spirit of the Fish (Aboriginal Tribes, Australia)

Across the vast landscapes of Australia, Aboriginal tribes have long held a deep spiritual connection with the natural world, including the creatures that inhabit it. Fishing tales from these tribes often involve shamans who possess the power to communicate with the spirit of the fish. It is said that the shamans would specifically choose a single fish to catch, and through a series of chants and rituals, they would lure the chosen fish to their nets. While this might seem like a mere myth, there are anecdotes passed down through generations that speak of successful encounters between the shamans and their intended catch. These tales exemplify the profound reverence Aboriginal tribes hold for nature and their remarkable spiritual connection.

From the Great Plains of North America to the remote Aboriginal tribes in Australia, fishing anecdotes have played a significant role in shaping the cultural fabric of countless civilizations. These stories not only entertain but also provide valuable insights into the human connection with nature. Despite our modern advancements, the tales of cunning tricksters, mythical creatures, spiritual encounters, and divine punishments continue to remind us of the timeless bond between humanity and the age-old pursuit of fishing. As we navigate the ever-changing world, these anecdotes serve as a testament to the intrinsic value of cultural and historical fishing tales, preserving the captivating narratives that have been passed down from generation to generation.

A Tapestry of Angling Experiences

Angling, the art and practice of fishing, has been captivating the hearts and minds of humans for centuries. From casting a line into crystal-clear streams to embarking on deep sea adventures, the pursuit of fish has woven a mesmerizing tapestry of experiences for anglers worldwide. In this chapter, we embark on a journey through different fishing adventures, exploring the rich and diverse world that angling offers. Join us as we delve into the stories, techniques, and emotions that make angling an enduring passion.

Fly Fishing: A Dance with Nature:

Fly fishing, with its graceful casts and intimate connection to the natural world, holds a special place in the hearts of many anglers. Standing knee-deep in a babbling brook, surrounded by verdant forests, the fly angler becomes one with the elements. With delicate precision, a fly is carefully chosen to mimic nature, and in a gentle motion, it takes flight. The angler watches with bated breath as the fly floats effortlessly on the water's surface, waiting for that elusive trout to rise.

But fly fishing is not just about catching fish; it's about the experience. It's about the anticipation of the strike, the feel of the tug, and the connection to a pristine environment. It's about moments of solitude, interrupted only by the song of birds and the rustle of leaves. Fly fishing is an art form—a dance between angler and nature, where the lines blur, and time stands still.

Big Game Fishing: Battling Giants of the Deep:

For those seeking a more adrenaline-fueled angling experience, big game fishing presents an unparalleled thrill. Picture a sleek boat cutting through the open ocean, its wake trailing behind like a white ribbon on a canvas of blue. The anticipation in the air is palpable as anglers prepare their massive rods and reels for battle. The heavy-duty line zings through the air, casting a baited hook far into the depths below.

Then it happens—a mighty strike, the rod bends in an arc, and the reel screams its protest. The angler, muscles straining, engages in an intense contest of strength and skill. The fish fights for its life, testing the angler's determination. This is a battle where neither participant gives in easily. Moments turn into hours as the angler desperately fights the powerful creature, and finally, after a grueling struggle, the prize breaks through the surface—an enormous marlin, its sparkling scales reflecting the sun's brilliance.

Ice Fishing: Braving the Frozen Domain:

When winter blankets the land in a thick layer of snow and ice, some anglers embark on a unique adventure—ice fishing. Armed with augers, tip-ups, and warm layers, they venture onto frozen lakes in search of fish hidden beneath the icy surface. With a rhythmic thud, the angler drills a hole through the thick ice, revealing a portal into a mysterious underwater world.

Wrapped in the solitude of the frozen domain, the angler's patience becomes paramount. Motionlessly, they sit, occasionally checking lines for a telltale tug or nibble. Days spent ice fishing are filled with quiet reflection, interspersed with moments of exhilaration when a fish takes the bait. In these frozen landscapes, anglers find solace, peace, and a connection to nature that transcends the biting cold.

Saltwater Shore Fishing: Dancing with Tides:

For those who prefer the hustle and bustle of the seashore, saltwater shore fishing is the perfect choice. Casting their lines from rocky outcrops or sandy beaches, anglers tackle the ever-changing tides, harnessing the rhythm of the ocean. With the crashing waves as their backdrop, they embrace a sense of adventure and unpredictability.

Whether it's surfcasting for striped bass on the Eastern shores of the United States or chasing snapper along the Australian coastline, saltwater shore fishing provides an opportunity to connect with the powerful forces of the sea. The angler feels the salt spray on their face and breathes in the briny air, while their eyes scan the horizon for any signs of feeding fish. With the backdrop of crashing waves, the angler's hopes rise and fall with each cast, creating indelible memories and stories that stretch beyond the boundaries of a single day.

In Angling is not merely about the fish caught but the experiences lived. Through fly fishing, anglers find harmony with nature, casting delicate lines and watching them dance through crystal-clear waters. In the battle of big game fishing, they test their strength against the giants of the deep, forging a connection to the untamed elements. Ice fishing reveals a quiet and tranquil world of frozen beauty, echoing with the sounds of solitude. On saltwater shores, anglers embrace the ebb and flow of the tides, their fishing journeys intertwined with the restless movements of the sea.

In this chapter, we have explored just a few of the countless angling experiences that exist, each with its own unique rhythm and allure. Angling captures the essence of our human connection to nature, embodying patience, determination, and a reverence for the wild. So, whether you cast a line in a babbling brook, an icy lake, or out into the vast ocean, remember that angling is more than a sport—it is a tapestry that weaves our souls with the vastness of the natural world.

Chapter 10: Cooking and Savoring the Catch

After successfully reeling in your prized catch, the next step in your fishing adventure is to transform that fresh seafood into a mouthwatering culinary masterpiece. Chapter 10 of our book, "The Angler's Guide: Mastering the Art of Fishing," delves into the art of cooking and savoring the catch to elevate your fishing experience to new heights. In this chapter, we will explore various techniques, recipes, and tips to ensure you make the most of your bountiful harvest. So, grab your apron and prepare to embark on a gastronomic journey like no other!

1. From Ocean to Plate:

As an angler, you possess a unique opportunity to feast on the freshest seafood imaginable. To truly savor the catch, it is essential to handle and store the fish properly. Firstly, aim to clean and gut your fish as soon as possible after catching them. This ensures the quality and flavor are preserved while preventing any undesirable odors. Utilizing the right tools, such as sharp knives and a clean workspace, will make this task a breeze.

Once the fish are properly cleaned, chilling them on ice or in a refrigerated cooler will help maintain freshness until it is time to prepare your meal. Quick tip: placing damp newspaper or towels inside the cooler will help keep the fish cool without allowing them to become waterlogged.

2. Selecting the Right Cooking Method:

The method you choose to cook your catch greatly impacts its flavor and texture. There are numerous techniques at your disposal, each suited to different types of seafood. Some popular methods include grilling, frying, baking, steaming, and even raw preparations like ceviche. To ensure you make the most of your catch, it is essential to match the cooking method to the species and cut of fish.

For firm, meaty fish such as swordfish or tuna, grilling or broiling is an excellent option. The high heat helps to sear the exterior while keeping the center moist and flavorful. Delicate white fish, like sole or flounder, are best when pan-fried or steamed to preserve their tender texture. Experimentation is key here, as each species may have different cooking requirements. Don't be afraid to try new methods and discover your favorite ways to prepare your catch.

3. Enhancing the Flavors:

While fresh fish can be delectable on its own, adding complementary flavors elevates the eating experience. Seasoning, marinades, sauces, and glazes all have an important role to play in amplifying the taste of your catch. Let's delve into some essential techniques to enhance the flavors of your culinary creation.

Seasoning: Simple ingredients like salt, pepper, and herbs can work wonders in bringing out the natural flavors of the fish. A sprinkle of seafood seasoning or a squeeze of lemon juice can complement the subtle taste of most fish species.

Marinades: Marinating fish before cooking is a great way to infuse it with flavors. Citrus-based marinades, like lime or orange, are particularly fantastic for white fish fillets. For heartier fish, you might try marinating with soy or teriyaki sauce to add depth and complexity.

Sauces and Glazes: Once your fish is cooked, a well-paired sauce or glaze can be the final touch to perfection. Creamy dill sauce pairs wonderfully with salmon, while a tangy tartar sauce complements crispy fried fish beautifully. Experimenting with different sauces allows you to explore a world of flavors.

4. Recipes to Delight:

Now that we've covered the basics, let's dive into some mouthwatering recipes to inspire your culinary journey with the catch of the day.

Recipe 1: Grilled Swordfish Steaks with Lemon-Herb Butter

Ingredients:
- 4 swordfish steaks (1 inch thick)
- 4 tablespoons unsalted butter, softened

- Zest of 1 lemon

- 1 tablespoon chopped fresh parsley

- Salt and pepper to taste

Instructions:

1. Preheat grill to medium-high heat.

2. In a small bowl, combine the softened butter, lemon zest, chopped parsley, salt, and pepper.

3. Season the swordfish steaks with salt and pepper on both sides.

4. Place the steaks on the grill and cook for 4-5 minutes per side, or until the fish is opaque and firm to the touch.

5. Remove the swordfish steaks from the grill and top each with a dollop of the lemon-herb butter.

6. Allow the butter to melt slightly and serve immediately alongside a fresh green salad.

Recipe 2: Pan-Fried Red Snapper with Mango Salsa

Ingredients:

- 4 red snapper fillets

- 2 tablespoons olive oil

- 1 teaspoon smoked paprika

- Salt and pepper to taste

Mango Salsa:

- 1 ripe mango, peeled and diced

- 1 small red onion, finely chopped

- 1 jalapeno pepper, seeds removed and finely chopped (optional)

- Juice of 1 lime

- 2 tablespoons chopped fresh cilantro

- Salt to taste

Instructions:

1. In a small bowl, combine all the ingredients for the mango salsa and set aside.

2. Rinse the snapper fillets and pat them dry with a paper towel.

3. Season the fillets with salt, pepper, and smoked paprika on both sides.

4. Heat the olive oil in a large skillet over medium-high heat.

5. Place the snapper fillets into the pan and cook for 3-4 minutes per side, or until the flesh is opaque and flakes easily.

6. Once cooked, remove the fillets from the pan and place them on a serving plate.

7. Spoon the mango salsa over the top of each fillet and serve immediately with steamed rice or roasted vegetables.

Chapter 10 has provided you with valuable insights into the art of cooking and savoring the catch. Remember, the journey doesn't end with landing the fish; it is just the beginning of a gastronomic adventure. From choosing the right cooking method to enhancing flavors with seasonings and sauces, these tips and recipes will help you create memorable seafood dishes that showcase your angling prowess. So, roll up your sleeves, sharpen your knives, and embark on a culinary expedition that celebrates your love for fishing and the bountiful rewards it brings.

From Water to Table: Handling Freshness

Fresh seafood is a culinary delight that promises a burst of flavors and an unparalleled dining experience. Whether it's succulent shrimp, tender fish fillets, or tantalizing lobster, there's no denying that seafood holds a special place in our hearts and on our plates. But have you ever wondered how this delectable bounty from the sea makes its way onto our tables while maintaining its freshness and quality? In this chapter, we will delve deep into the intricate process of handling seafood freshness, from the moment it is harvested from the water until it reaches our kitchens.

The Journey Begins: Harvesting the Sea's Treasures

Picture a group of fishermen heading out into the vast expanse of the ocean, their boats slicing through the waves in search of a bountiful catch. As the early morning sun breaks the horizon, they drop their nets or lines into the water, ready to reel in their fine treasures. This initial step, the harvest, is crucial in ensuring that the seafood is of the highest quality.

When it comes to capturing seafood, there are various methods employed depending on the type of species being targeted. Some fishermen use trawling nets to catch fish in bulk, while others opt for longlines, traps, or even handpicking certain species. Regardless of the method, the aim is to minimize stress on the fish, ensuring they are brought aboard swiftly and efficiently.

To maintain optimal freshness, it is essential to keep the catch chilled immediately after harvesting. On modern fishing vessels, this is usually achieved by using ice or refrigeration systems, which help preserve the quality of the seafood during transportation.

Icy Immersion: The Art of Keeping Seafood Fresh

Once the catch is safely on board, a well-rehearsed routine begins to ensure the seafood's freshness is preserved. Any fish or shellfish that is still alive is transferred to specially designed holding tanks filled with chilled seawater. These tanks mimic the natural habitat of the seafood and prevent overcrowding, allowing the creatures to swim freely and remain healthy until they reach the shore.

While some species can survive outside of water for longer periods, maintaining a cold and moist environment is vital in preventing stress and deterioration of the seafood's quality. The use of recirculating systems and temperature controls in these holding tanks ensures that the water remains at the optimal temperature for the specific species being caught, further enhancing the overall freshness of the seafood.

From Vessel to Shore: Handling with Care

After hours or even days at sea, the fishing vessel finally returns to the shore, laden with buckets brimming with the day's catch. The meticulous process of preserving freshness doesn't stop here; it continues with the careful handling of the seafood as it is unloaded from the boat.

The catch is usually transferred onto ice-filled containers or directly into refrigerated trucks for transportation to processing facilities or local markets. It is important to note that maintaining a consistently cold temperature throughout this step ensures that the seafood's freshness is not compromised. To achieve this, many fishing vessels are equipped with onboard ice-making facilities, guaranteeing a steady supply of ice throughout the journey.

Processing and Value Addition: Bringing Out the Best
Upon reaching the processing facilities, the seafood undergoes various steps to further enhance its quality, appearance, and taste. This stage involves cleaning, shucking, scaling, filleting, and packaging, depending on the type of seafood being processed. Unwanted parts, such as the fish heads, shells, or innards, are carefully removed to eliminate any unpleasant flavors or odors. Filleting machines skillfully slice through fish bodies, yielding perfectly portioned fillets that are ready to be processed further or sent directly to market. Freshness is maintained throughout the processing by ensuring proper temperature controls and using high-grade packaging materials that prevent any contamination or loss of quality.

Transportation: A Race Against Time
Once the seafood has undergone the necessary processing steps, it is time for it to embark on its journey to local markets or global destinations. Efficient transportation is crucial to maintain optimal freshness, as seafood is highly perishable and can deteriorate rapidly if not handled properly.
Refrigerated trucks or shipping containers fitted with advanced

cooling mechanisms are commonly used to transport seafood over long distances. These vehicles maintain a consistent temperature, typically between 32°F and 39°F (0°C and 4°C), to prevent bacterial growth and prolong shelf life. The containers are carefully sealed to create a controlled environment that protects the seafood from exposure to external factors such as temperature fluctuations, humidity, and unwanted odors.

Market Arrival: Ensuring Quality for Consumers

Upon arrival at local markets or restaurants, the responsibility of ensuring the seafood's freshness is passed on to the retailers and chefs. It is crucial for these professionals to continue the proper handling and storage practices to deliver the finest seafood to their customers.

Retailers often display seafood on ice beds to maintain a cool temperature and help preserve freshness. Careful rotation and monitoring of stock are vital to ensure older seafood is sold first, avoiding any waste. In restaurants, chefs meticulously inspect and handle the seafood, choosing the freshest options for their dishes. They store it properly, using refrigerators or ice to maintain optimal conditions until it is time to cook and serve.

Handling seafood freshness from the water to the table is an art that requires the concerted efforts of fishermen, processors, transportation specialists, retailers, and chefs. Each step along the journey contributes to delivering the highest quality and freshest seafood possible to consumers worldwide. By understanding and appreciating this intricate process, we can savor each bite of our favorite seafood dish, knowing that it has traveled a long and careful journey to reach our plates.

Celebrating the Culinary Diversity of Fish

Fish, often hailed as the "fruit of the sea," has been an essential component of human diets for centuries. From the freshwater lakes to the vast oceans, fish have provided sustenance and nourishment to communities across the globe. Not only are they a rich source of protein, but they also offer a variety of essential nutrients and omega-3 fatty acids, making them a preferred choice for health-conscious individuals. However, beyond their nutritional value, fish also possess an incredible diversity of flavors, textures, and culinary potentials that have captured the imagination of chefs and food enthusiasts worldwide. In this chapter, we delve into the fascinating world of fish and explore the countless ways in which their culinary diversity can be celebrated.

1. The Perfection of Simplicity:

One of the great joys of fish is its ability to shine in simple preparations, allowing its natural flavors to take center stage. Whether grilled, pan-seared, or poached, a fresh piece of fish requires little embellishment to create a masterful dish. In Mediterranean cuisine, fresh whole fish, grilled with just a drizzle of olive oil, a sprinkle of sea salt, and a squeeze of lemon, showcases the delicate flavors of the sea. Simple yet stunning, this dish pays homage to the natural goodness of fish.

2. From Mediterranean Waters to Your Plate:

Each region of the world brings forth its unique culinary traditions when it comes to celebrating fish. The Mediterranean, with its rich history and diverse coastline, offers a myriad of preparations that highlight the freshness and vibrancy of the catch. From Spanish paella adorned with an assortment of fish and shellfish to Italian cioppino, a robust fish stew bursting with tomatoes, herbs, and garlic, the Mediterranean's love affair with fish knows no bounds. The bright flavors and colorful presentations transport diners to the sun-drenched shores where these dishes originated.

3. Southeast Asian Sensations:

Traveling east, we encounter Southeast Asia, a region renowned for its bold and vibrant flavors. Here, fish finds its place in a variety of dishes, including curries, soups, and stir-fries. Take the Thai dish "Pla Rad Prik," or deep-fried fish with chili sauce, as an example. The contrast between the crispiness of the fish and the fiery chili-based sauce creates a harmonious balance of textures and flavors. In Indonesia, the iconic dish "Ikan Bakar," or grilled fish slathered with spicy sambal, tantalizes taste buds with its smoky and spicy attributes. The Southeast Asian culinary repertoire proves that fish has an extraordinary ability to soak up complex and fragrant spices, making each bite a delightful adventure.

4. Sushi: The Art of Raw Fish:

No exploration of fish culinary diversity would be complete without mentioning sushi, the epitome of exquisite and delectable raw fish preparations. Originating in Japan, sushi has become a global obsession, appealing to both the adventurous and the purist palates. From simple yet elegant nigiri, featuring a slice of raw fish atop a mound of vinegared rice, to the elaborate and creative maki rolls, sushi offers endless possibilities for both taste and presentation. The delicate balance of flavors, textures, and aesthetics in each perfectly crafted piece of sushi exemplifies the artistry and attention to detail devoted to this culinary tradition.

5. The Unsung Heroes: Lesser-Known Fish:

While popular fish varieties such as salmon and tuna often steal the spotlight, it's important to celebrate the culinary diversity of lesser-known species. Each region has its own hidden gems that offer unique flavors and textures waiting to be discovered. In Northern Europe, smoked herring takes center stage, providing a rich, smoky taste that has captivated generations. In South America, the Brazilian dish "Moqueca" showcases lesser-known fish such as tambaqui or pirarucu, creating a rich and fragrant fish stew with coconut milk, tomatoes, peppers, and cilantro. Exploring these lesser-known fish empowers us to expand our culinary horizons while supporting sustainable fishing practices.

6. A Sustainable Seafood Future:

As we celebrate the culinary diversity of fish, we must also address the importance of sustainability. Overfishing and destructive fishing practices threaten the delicate ecosystems that support fish populations. The celebration of fish must be accompanied by responsible fishing and sourcing practices to ensure the availability of these culinary treasures for future generations. By supporting sustainable seafood choices, we can protect both the biodiversity of our oceans and the pleasures of our palates.

Fish offers an unparalleled culinary diversity that spans continents and cultures. From the simplicity of a perfectly grilled fillet to the complex flavors of Southeast Asian curries, fish has the remarkable ability to satisfy our taste buds and nourish our bodies. By celebrating the countless ways fish can be prepared and enjoyed, we contribute to the preservation of centuries-old culinary traditions while embracing the future of sustainability. So, let us embark on a journey through the culinary seas, embracing the captivating flavors and textures that fish brings to our plates, and appreciating the interconnectedness between humans and the aquatic world.

Basic to Gourmet: Preparing Your Catch

There's no greater feeling for an angler than reeling in a fresh catch after hours spent patiently waiting by the water. For many, the excitement doesn't end there. The true joy lies in the process of transforming that well-earned catch into a mouthwatering, memorable meal. Whether you're a novice or an experienced angler, this chapter will guide you through the journey of turning your catch into culinary creations that range from simple and satisfying to truly gourmet. Grab your knives, sharpen your skills, and prepare to dive into a world of flavors!

Section 1: The Basics

1.1 Selecting the Freshest Fish:

The key to any successful seafood dish is starting with the freshest fish possible. Look for shiny skin, bright eyes, and a clean, fresh smell. Avoid fish with dull or cloudy eyes, mushy flesh, or a pungent odor.

1.2 Cleaning and Gutting your Catch:

Before diving into the culinary adventure, you must first prepare your catch. Rinse the fish under cold water, removing any scales with a sharp knife or a scaler. To gut the fish, make an incision from the tail to the base of the gills, and carefully remove the innards, rinsing the cavity thoroughly. Pat the fish dry with a paper towel before proceeding.

1.3 Filleting and Scaling:

To fillet your fish, start by making a diagonal cut just behind the gills towards the backbone. Then, glide your knife along the backbone, slowly separating the fillet from the body. Repeat the process on the other side. If you prefer to keep the skin on, scale the fillet using a scaler or the back of your knife. Starting from the tail, press the scaler against the skin and scrape it towards the head.

Section 2: Taking it Up a Notch - Intermediate Techniques

2.1 Moist and Flavorful Poaching:

Poaching is a gentle cooking method that keeps fish tender and moist. Place your fillets in a saucepan, cover them with a flavorful liquid, such as stock, wine, or a combination of both, and add aromatic ingredients like herbs, lemon slices, and spices. Bring the liquid to a gentle simmer and cook for 8-10 minutes until the fish is opaque and easily flakes with a fork.

2.2 Sautéing to Perfection:

Sautéing is a quick and versatile cooking technique that adds a delightful crispness to your fish fillets. Heat a bit of oil or butter in a skillet over medium-high heat. Season the fillets with salt and pepper, then place them skin-side down in the hot skillet. Cook for 3-4 minutes, until the skin becomes crispy, then carefully flip the fillets and cook for an additional 2-3 minutes until the fish is cooked through.

2.3 Grilling Techniques:

Grilling is a beloved method of preparing fish, imparting a delightful smoky flavor while allowing for endless flavor possibilities. Preheat your grill to medium-high heat and lightly oil the grates to prevent sticking. Place the fillets directly on the grill, skin-side down, and cook with the lid closed for 4-5 minutes. Carefully flip the fillets using a spatula and cook for an additional 2-3 minutes until the fish is opaque and easily flakes.

Section 3: Taking it to the Next Level - Advanced Techniques

3.1 The Art of Curing:

Curing fish intensifies flavors and gives a unique texture to your catch. For a basic cure, mix equal parts salt and sugar, and coat your fish fillets evenly. Add herbs, spices, or citrus zest for additional depth of flavor. Place the fillets in a shallow dish, cover with plastic wrap, and refrigerate for at least 24 hours. Rinse off the curing mixture before using in your preferred dish.

3.2 Complex Flavors through Marination:

Marinating fish infuses it with tantalizing flavors and tenderizes the flesh. Create a marinade by combining ingredients such as soy sauce, citrus juice, spices, herbs, and olive oil. Place your fish fillets in a shallow dish, pour the marinade over them, and refrigerate for at least 30 minutes, or up to a few hours for a more intense flavor. Remove the fillets from the marinade, pat them dry, and cook using your preferred method.

3.3 Spectacular Seafood Stocks:

Maximize the flavors of your fish by utilizing homemade seafood stocks. Simmer fish bones, shells, aromatic vegetables, and herbs in water to extract their rich flavors. Use the resulting stock as a base for soups, stews, sauces, or to poach your fillets. The depth of flavor achieved through homemade stocks will elevate your dishes to gourmet levels.

Embarking on the journey of turning your catch into culinary masterpieces opens up a world of possibilities. From basic techniques to advanced culinary skills, this chapter has provided you with the tools to prepare fish dishes that range from simple and satisfying to chef-worthy gourmet creations. Don your apron, gather your ingredients, and let the flavors of the sea guide you to extraordinary dining experiences. But remember, the true magic lies not only in the techniques but also in the passion and love you infuse into every dish you create. Happy cooking!